"Franciscan Albert Haase has done it again. *Coming Home to Your True Self* will receive a . . . warm reception from his readers, since it is steeped in the mystical tradition of the West from the Christian Scriptures to the desert dwellers of Egypt, and then through the Franciscans and the Dominicans, especially Meister Eckhart, which is becoming so popular with those seeking God in journeys of faith and love. It is highly recommended to all who seek the one thing necessary."

BR. PATRICK HART, *O.C.S.O., Abbey of Gethsemani*

"This is practical and profound spiritual guidance! If we do not clarify some of these foundational issues, there will be no real flourishing in our search for God. Albert Haase makes very substantial ideas readable, personal and even adventuresome. What a good Franciscan!"

RICHARD ROHR, *O.F.M., Center for Action and Contemplation, author of* Everything Belongs

"Albert Haase has captured the simple essence of the spiritual life in this readable treatment that flows easily from Jesus' parable of the prodigal son. Illustrating his points with lively personal stories, Fr. Haase illuminates such classical spiritual terms as *detachment, discernment* and *penance,* making them live for the modern reader. He draws deeply on the teaching of Jesus and shows us how to 'come home' to our true selves. A fine guidebook for those who long for a deeper relationship with the Lord."

EMILIE GRIFFIN, *author of* Doors into Prayer: An Invitation

"It occurred to me while reading this lovely book that Albert Haase is a wise and seasoned Christian man. It comes through in page after page. This book is informed, insightful and practical, everything you want a book on spirituality to be. Haase knows the subject so well that he writes from the inside, making it simple and clear. *Coming Home to Your True Self* made me want to do what the title says—find my true self in God. But more than that, it helped me make progress to that end."

GERALD L. SITTSER, *author of* A Grace Disguised *and* Water from a Deep Well

"Haase is a wise and winsome guide for the spiritual life and his book is a helpful companion for the journey of coming home to the true self."

RUTH HALEY BARTON, *author of* Sacred Rhythms

COMING HOME
TO YOUR TRUE SELF

Leaving the Emptiness of False Attractions

Albert Haase, O.F.M.

Foreword by M. Robert Mulholland Jr.

IVP Books

An imprint of InterVarsity Press
Downers Grove, Illinois

InterVarsity Press
P.O. Box 1400, Downers Grove, IL 60515-1426
World Wide Web: www.ivpress.com
E-mail: email@ivpress.com

InterVarsity Press® is the book-publishing division of InterVarsity Christian Fellowship/USA®, a student movement active on campus at hundreds of universities, colleges and schools of nursing in the United States of America, and a member movement of the International Fellowship of Evangelical Students. For information about local and regional activities, write Public Relations Dept., InterVarsity Christian Fellowship/USA, 6400 Schroeder Rd., P.O. Box 7895, Madison, WI 53707-7895, or visit the IVCF website at <www.intervarsity.org>.

Scripture quotations, unless otherwise noted, are from the New Revised Standard Version of the Bible, copyright 1989 by the Division of Christian Education of the National Council of the Churches of Christ in the USA. Used by permission. All rights reserved.

A version of chapter four appeared as Albert Haase, O.F.M., "Guilt as a Lenten Guide to Holiness," St. Anthony Messenger Magazine, February 1996.

A version of chapter six appeared as Albert Haase, O.F.M., "Lenten Penance: Getting Back on Track," St. Anthony Messenger Magazine, February 1997.

A version of chapter eight appeared as Albert Haase, O.F.M., "Spiritual Direction: Honoring New Occasions of Grace," St. Anthony Messenger Magazine, November 2007.

Design: Cindy Kiple
Images: Howard Kingsnorth/Getty Images

ISBN 978-0-8308-3517-1

Printed in the United States of America ∞

Library of Congress Cataloging-in-Publication Data

Haase, Albert, 1955-
  Coming home to your true self: leaving the emptiness of false
  attractions/Albert Haase.
     p. cm.
  Includes bibliographical references.
  ISBN 978-0-8308-3517-1 (pbk.: alk. paper)
  1. Christian life. 2. Spirituality. I. Title.
  BV4501.3.H325 2008
  248.4—dc22
                                                                    2008005933

P	18	17	16	15	14	13	12	11	10	9	8	7	6	5	4	3	2	1
Y	23	22	21	20	19	18	17	16	15	14	13	12	11	10	09	08

Lovingly dedicated to my eldest sister,

Bridget Haase, O.S.U.,

who celebrates a homecoming

wherever she is

CONTENTS

"God is at home.

It is we who have gone out for a walk."

MEISTER ECKHART

FOREWORD

One of the great dangers in the contemporary renaissance of interest in Christian spirituality is that many people have no awareness of the rich heritage of two thousand years of Christian spirituality. This consequently gives rise to a plethora of "pop spiritualities."

Many of the popular "spirituality" books can lead us into dangerous grounds of unbiblical and heretical teachings. Or, at the least, they fail to provide the substance and depth that draw us closer to Christ. How can we reach into the deep levels of Christian spirituality?

True wisdom is drawn from the reaches of time-tested Christian tradition. The spiritual mothers and fathers of the tradition can guide us in the deeper journey while keeping us on a path of true faith.

A perennial problem, however, is that much of this classic literature is relatively inaccessible to those beginning their spiritual pilgrimage, often even for those well along the road. The church fathers and mothers used images, symbols, metaphors and frames of reference which resonated with readers in their day, but which largely fail to connect with us.

In this book we have a resource for Christian spirituality that effectively taps the wealth of the Christian spiritual tradition in a way that makes it accessible to contemporary readers. Albert Haase has reframed the essential dynamics of the spiritual journey to connect powerfully with the contemporary age. And through the reflection questions at the close of each chapter, he helps us connect the material to our own journey as well.

Even as this book brings the riches of tradition to the most intimate aspects of our lives with Christ, there's something more important that this book reflects: the essential purpose of the spiritual journey is a life of other-referenced love. Through an abundance of real-life examples, Haase shows us how we live our spirituality in relationship with others.

I believe *Coming Home to Your True Self* will be a significant blessing for those who hunger for a genuine spiritual journey.

M. Robert Mulholland Jr.
Kingdomtide 2007

PREFACE

In the late 1980s, I started giving lectures and workshops on prayer and the spiritual life. Though they were well received, it quickly became evident that the majority of people did not fully appreciate the images and language that were often bound to a different time, place, culture and theology. Some people found the teachings of the mystics old-fashioned, while others thought they catered to people living behind monastery walls, who did not have the daily challenge of raising children or working a nine-to-five job. In hindsight, the majority were right. We needed a contemporary way to talk about the spiritual insights of the past.

Before leaving for missionary activity in mainland China, I attended a ten-day centering prayer workshop under Abbot Thomas Keating at the Trappist monastery in Snowmass, Colorado. That experience planted seeds that would grow during my eleven and a half years in China. Those who know Keating's approach to the spiritual life will recognize his strong influence on my understanding of spiritual formation.

Soon after my return to the United States in early 2004, I was asked to give a workshop on the spiritual life at Quincy University in Quincy, Illinois. This time I was intent on making the riches of the Christian spiritual tradition more accessible to the participants. That request gave rise to "Like the Air We Breathe: An Approach to the Spiritual Life," a workshop I have since presented to hundreds of clergy, religious sisters and laity. Thanks to the encouragement of those participants and the kind offer of InterVarsity Press, I am now honored to present the content of that workshop in written form to a wider audience.

Coming Home to Your True Self uses a line once preached by Meister Eckhart, the great Dominican mystic of the fourteenth century, as an interpretive key to Jesus' parable of the prodigal son (see Luke 15:11-32). "God is at home. It is we who have gone out for a walk." Combined with my understanding of the true self and the false self, it presents the spiritual journey as a return home. And home is the sacrament of the present moment. It is only in living right now, right here, that we discover our lives and this world awash in the grace of God. We can actually be loading the dishwasher or sitting in a board meeting and still experience what the great spiritual mystics discovered behind monastery walls.

The key points of this book are summarized in outline form in appendix C. After reading this book, a periodic review of this appendix can help keep the ideas alive and the challenges ongoing. Spiritual formation requires a daily and seasonal commitment.

A quick glance at the contents page and the appendix reveals that we are invited to a homecoming. We have lost our true selves and have gone on a wild-goose chase after false attractions that drive us into a pigpen in a foreign land. We need to come back home and be the people God created us to be.

This book, in discussing how guilt, prayer, penance, discernment, spiritual direction and the process of spiritual growth can help us get back home, offers a contemporary approach to spiritual formation that translates the revered teachings of the past into the language of the twenty-first century. The questions at the end of each chapter are intended for personal reflection or interaction with a spiritual director or other spiritual friend. If you want to use the book with a group, you may want to adapt them to fit your needs.

You will meet many people in these pages whose names and personal details have been changed. Each has graciously agreed to allow me to share the story of God's grace in his or her life.

Heartfelt thanks to the staff of Mayslake Ministries in Westmont, Illinois, for tolerating all my monkeyshines, encouraging my ideas and giving me a place to hang my friar's hood. It's a real joy to collaborate with people who are committed to adult spiritual formation, the ancient practice of spiritual direction and the challenge of preaching the Word of God in and out of season.

I am grateful to the Franciscan friars of the Sacred Heart Province, living and deceased, as well as former friars, who have challenged me and loved me to this present moment in my life. The present moment is sacramental not only because of the love I find here but also because of the love that gets me here.

What can I say about my eldest sister, Bridget Haase, O.S.U., to whom this book is dedicated? She never winces when I ask her to read my gobbledygook. And I chuckle as she reminds me that English is, in fact, my first language. Sometimes, while writing, I forget that.

I am humbled by the generous foreword written by Dr. M. Robert Mulholland Jr. I heartily recommend his wonderful book *Invitation to a Journey: A Road Map for Spiritual Formation.*

Special thanks to Fr. John Breslin, Deacon Bruce McElrath and the entire congregation of St. Ailbe Catholic Church, Chicago. Located at the corner of Ninety-First Street and Stony Island Avenue, it's a place where "you can be whoever you want to be," as the pastor is fond of saying. But don't miss the point: anyone and everyone is welcomed. St. Ailbe's is truly a place that reflects the open arms of our loving God.

Thanks as well to LaVonne Neff, who read the original manuscript and offered helpful suggestions for the book's improvement.

And finally, I would like to thank Marilyn Stewart, a member of the board of directors of Mayslake Ministries, and Cindy Bunch, senior book editor at InterVarsity Press. They are the ones who initially thought that the words of a Franciscan priest might be helpful to another audience.

It is my prayer that all of us never grow weary of trying to come home to the sacrament of the present moment. For in the end, there's nowhere else to go. And more importantly, there is, in fact, nowhere else to be.

Albert Haase, O.F.M.
Feast of the Annunciation

1

THE TRUE SELF

Home Sweet Home

Mom and Dad just called from the hospital. They're bringing the new baby home in about two hours. They told me to call you and invite you over to see him."

I could hear the excitement in eight-year-old Jason's voice. He seemed thrilled to have a baby brother.

I finished what I was doing and then headed over to the Carpenters' home. Within twenty minutes of my arrival, Jason and I heard the car pull into the driveway. He ran to the front door to open it. I stood a few steps behind him.

After a few minutes, Luke and Katie got out of the car. Luke was carrying a bundle in his arms. Jason and I were both aware that it was the newborn baby.

Once inside the door, Luke asked Jason, "Do you want to see your baby brother, Aiden Alexander?" Jason's face betrayed his joy and curiosity.

I watched as Luke carefully unwrapped layer upon layer of blankets. Jason got his first look at his new brother.

"Father, please!" Luke said, motioning for me to hold the newborn. I carefully laid little Aiden in a cradle made of my right arm and looked into his tiny, pink face. He was sound asleep, his eyelids just slightly ajar. A heavy silence descended on me as I stared in awe-filled wonder and recalled how my grandmother used to say that newborns "dream about the angels." There was something truly celestial about this three-day-old infant. I felt myself holding back tears of disbelief. *It truly is a miracle,* I said to myself. Another human life had come into the world. Time stood still as my stare became a contemplative gaze on a totally content, dependent newborn who, at that very moment, radiated the presence of God.

Luke bent over my shoulder and whispered to little Aiden, "Welcome home!" That greeting instantly reminded me that I too had returned to where I belong.

WELCOME HOME!

There are times in life when the present moment opens up like doors to a magnificent homecoming party. Everything converges on a single, simple point—a newborn infant, a waterfall, the pronouncement of wedding vows, an experience of deep silence in the present moment, a selfless kiss.

This moment catches the rays of the sun through a magnifying glass and burns a hole in our memory. We remember everything about it: the weather, the music playing in the background, the people around us.

We are wide awake and truly *live* this moment with attentive awareness. We transcend "me" as our attention is riveted on "thee" (others)—whatever that might be. In such moments, Luke's words ring loudly and clearly: "Welcome home!"

Down through the centuries, Christians have considered such

selfless moments spiritual. They can be quite dramatic; they can be quite ordinary. While meditating on the passion of Christ, Francis of Assisi had an experience of the crucified Christ that left physical wounds in his flesh. Julian of Norwich, a great woman mystic of fourteenth-century England, saw the unity of the universe in a small hazelnut held in the palm of her hand. Sixteenth-century mystic John of the Cross used paradoxical language and spoke of an interior darkness that dazzled with a spiritual light. In 1600, Jakob Boehme, while working in his cobbler's shop, saw the light of the sun reflected in a tin vessel and instantly realized that true knowledge of God brings a person into the light. Brother Lawrence of the Resurrection, a seventeenth-century cook of the Carmelite Order, experienced God while making an omelet. On a Wednesday evening in May 1738, John Wesley, while listening to someone reflect on Luther's "Preface to the Letter of St. Paul to the Romans," felt his heart "strangely warmed" and justified in the sight of God. With loving attentiveness, Mother Teresa of Calcutta ministered to the dying and, in them, discovered the presence of the crucified, thirsty Jesus. Different times, different people, different experiences—but the same discovery of the divine Presence in the present moment.

A spiritual experience within the Judeo-Christian tradition is focused on "Thee," the divine Presence, often mediated through "thee," another person or object. Rather than broadening self-awareness, it broadens God-awareness and is initiated by God. Indeed, it is a grace, a gift. At times, God mysteriously inches into our lives like the morning tide or a tiny whisper. One thinks of Elijah outside the cave (see 1 Kings 19:9-13). At other times, the Presence comes out of nowhere, commanding attention, wonder and awe as God did with Moses in the burning bush (see Exodus 3:1-6) or Jesus with his three disciples on Mount Tabor (see Matthew 17:1-8).

In such moments and experiences, our attention is riveted on the present moment as an interior door is thrown open in welcome. We find ourselves invited into a mysterious darkness pregnant with the loving divine Presence. We are taken by the hand and led to a place that feels all too familiar and yet is strangely new. At such times, we are welcomed home.

Become Like a Child

Without realizing it, Luke had spoken a deep spiritual truth to little Aiden when he said, "Welcome home!" Aiden truly was home, but in a sense deeper than a sociologist's understanding of a family unit. Like any other infant, he could live only in the present, for he had yet to learn of something called "the past" and "the future." When awake, Aiden would gradually learn to focus on everything that surrounded him. He would be totally dependent on Luke and Katie for all his needs. And if my grandmother was correct, he would dream of the angels, indicative of the presence of God that surrounded him and radiated through his very presence. Indeed, Aiden was home. He was right where he belonged and where God intended and created him to be. He was living in the here and now.

This focused and dependent disposition, so evident in newborn infants, is analogous to what some spiritual writers refer to as the true self. The true self experiences, lives in and responds to the present moment. It is attentive to the divine Presence right here, right now, as it comes to us under the guise of a living person, some inanimate form of creation or an event. With childlike simplicity and spontaneity, the true self is dependent and has a relationship with thee (others) in the here and now as the sacred place of encounter with Thee (God).

Perhaps that is why Jesus makes the bold proclamation, "Truly I tell you, unless you change and become like children, you will never enter the kingdom of heaven" (Matthew 18:3). We need to return to being who God created us to be and stop being who we are not. We need to come back home to the true self.

A little reality check speaks volumes about how far we have wandered away. Newborns, because they are focused on the present, do not experience the learned behaviors of guilt and sentimentality that are characteristics of the adult obsession with the past. Because they are focused on the present, newborns do not experience the learned behaviors of worry and anxiety that are characteristics of the adult obsession with the future. Guilt, sentimentality, worry and anxiety arise in our lives as we grow into adulthood.

A parent tosses his young daughter high into the air, and the child giggles with glee because she is certain that loving arms will be waiting to catch her on her descent. Her trust is natural and spontaneous. However, as that child becomes an adult, she will be conditioned toward independence and will soon learn how to be self-reliant and distrustful of others. With that, the natural God-given trust in others fades into memory.

The great tragedy for many of us is that in growing up, we become self-made, independent successes who are weighed down with thoughts of the past and worries about the future. We lose touch with our true self, the person God created us to be. We live off-center and alienated from who we really are.

THE GREAT INSIGHT

Our alienation is no more evident than in our experience of God. If little infants like Aiden do dream about the angels, then the divine Presence is naturally close to us. The history of Christian spirituality certainly attests to that. Indeed, the tradition speaks of a divine indwelling with expressions such as "interior fire," "the ground of my being," "the spark of the soul." Meister Eckhart preached, "God is at home," and home for him was within. Paul wrote to the Galatians, "It is no longer I who live, but it is Christ who lives in me" (Galatians 2:20). At the very core of our being, whether we are conscious of it or not, there is a communion—a "common union"—with God. In the words of Catherine of Genoa, "My me is God!"

And this divine Presence is not simply some objective "thing" inside us. The divine Presence also surrounds us like the air we breathe. Apparently quoting a Greek poet, Paul preached at the Areopagus, "In him we live and move and have our being" (Acts 17:28). The first letter of John makes clear that the divine Presence is the fishbowl in which lovers swim: "God is love, and those who abide in love abide in God, and God abides in them" (1 John 4:16).

Human language always stammers, limps and collapses when trying to express or communicate the mystery of God. Whatever is said or written about God will be off the mark and prone to misinterpretation and error. As Eckhart said, "The hand that writes the true thing about God is the hand that erases." Only silence and erased blackboards have the capacity to speak and convey the truth about God. And so we must be content with analogy and allegory when speaking of the divine Presence.

Thomas Merton once used the analogy of walking outside in the fresh air to speak of the experience of God. He said we usually do not concentrate on the fresh air—we simply breathe it. And we normally do not fix our attention on the sunlight—we simply enjoy and bask in it. And so, Merton said, the things that correspond to the divine Presence are not things on which we can and do concentrate. Rather, we simply are *in* them as we are *in* the divine Presence.

Many of us ask, "Where is God?" But that's like asking the location of air or the direction of sunlight. The divine Presence is not a "thing" that is "out there." Lovers abide in God and God in them. "For then the soul is in God and God in the soul just as the fish is in the sea and the sea in the fish," Catherine of Siena wrote.

Using John of the Cross's analogy of a window pane and light, we can say that our physical bodies and our historical lives are stained-glass windows through which the interior presence of God—the divine light—shines to the world. As we read in the Gospel of Matthew, "Let your light shine before others, so that they may see your good works and give glory to your Father in heaven" (5:16). We are sacraments, tabernacles of the living God. That awareness of Thee is the key to the door of this very moment. And it is right here, right now, where God intends for us to be.

Of course, this points to the great insight: there is nothing to "get" in the spiritual life because we already have it! We simply need to become aware of the Presence who dwells within and in whom we dwell. We need to be attentive to the sacrament of the present moment.

Every time I get into an automobile, I look at those words printed on the bottom of the passenger side-view mirror: "Objects in mirror are closer than they appear." That speaks of the divine Presence. God is closer to us than we have ever imagined or dreamt. Genesis portrays Adam and Eve experiencing the divine Presence in the evening breeze (see Genesis 3:8). Augustine of Hippo said, "God is closer to your soul than you are yourself." Indeed, to quote Eckhart again, "God is at home."

THE INCARNATION

Of course, this insight is hard for us Westerners to accept. As we grow up and are trained in the dualistic thinking of our culture, we quickly learn to divide and compartmentalize our lives. God is up there and we are down here. As a Scripture scholar once commented, we live and work in one world while believing and praying in another. Surprisingly, the God of the Christian turns such thinking upside down and inside out.

Jews, Christians and Muslims all share the same one God and have a deep respect for divine transcendence. I remember watching Muslims in Cameroon, West Africa, as they pulled out their prayer mats, faced Mecca and began their prostrations and prayers to Allah. Muslims have a tremendous awareness of Allah's presence in their lives—they call it *taqwa*—and a deep respect for God's transcendence. They publicly call it to mind five times a day.

But it was while visiting a patient named Iridizo in the hospital run by the Franciscan sisters in the village of Shisong that I also realized the great difference between Christians and Muslims.

Black Muslim Iridizo had a lot of questions to ask the visiting white priest from faraway America: "Is it really true that in your country you have machines that make the air in buildings cold? Why would you ever want to do that? And why do you need so many different kinds of cars?"

After we discussed everything from air-conditioning to the American fascination with the automobile, our conversation inevitably turned to the topic of religion. I was surprised at Iridizo's directness: "When we Muslims get together to pray, we are very respectful toward Allah. We pray on special mats. We prostrate and bow. We love Allah dearly, and we show that by the way we pray.

But you Catholics are so different. I went to one of your services and was shocked to see people turning around and shaking hands. How do you show reverence and respect for the Compassionate One when everyone is shaking hands?"

Iridizo's question revealed the fundamental difference between Muslims and Christians. For Muslims, Allah lives in heaven and must be shown respect and reverence. For those who profess faith in Jesus, however, the transcendent God "up there," in the words of the fourth Gospel, "became flesh and lived among us" (John 1:14). This is the wonder of Christmas: God has come down to earth in human flesh. He is Emmanuel, God with us.

Though language is inadequate to contain the truth of the divine, in the miracle of Christmas, God entered the only and most apt vessel that *can* contain the ineffable divine Presence: the tabernacle of human flesh. To borrow the imagery from Paul, there is a precious treasure found in the clay vessel of human flesh (see 2 Corinthians 4:7).

God's embrace of the body at Christmas is a dramatic event that radically affirms the goodness and sanctity of human flesh. Traditional piety has often evaded Paul's challenging reminder, "Or do you not know that your body is a temple of the Holy Spirit within you?" (1 Corinthians 6:19). God is most certainly at home. God is with us.

CHARACTERISTICS OF BEING HOME

How do we know if the true self is emerging? What are the characteristics of a person who is "at home" with God? What fruits are found in the life of someone who is aware of and celebrates the common union with God? Though the list is far from exhaustive, there are ten traits of people who have come home to the present moment where God intends them to be.

CHARACTERISTICS OF THE TRUE SELF

- Relational
- Self-giving
- Unflappable and unthreatened
- Focused on the here and now
- Contemplative approach to life
- Wonder and awe
- Trustful surrender
- Compassionate
- Awareness of being a spoke in the larger wheel of creation
- Passion for peace and justice

The first characteristic goes to the very heart of being created in the image and likeness of God. Since the First Council of Nicaea in 325, Christians have affirmed that God is a trinity of Persons: Father, Son and Spirit. The Father is only a father because he has a son. And the Son is only a son because he has a father. And they are in relationship because the Spirit binds them together. The point is obvious: the very essence of God—what makes the divine Presence divine—is God's relational nature. "God is love, and those who abide in love abide in God, and God abides in them" (1 John 4:16).

Those of us rooted in the true self are *relational*. We too foster and exist in a trinity of relationships between God, others and self. Just as dimensions of God's divinity are revealed in the relationships of the Trinity, dimensions of our humanity are discovered when we are in relationship with God and others. Indeed, only then do we discover who we really are: members of a family inextricably bound together—sharing a common union—because of the divine image and likeness stamped on our souls.

Christianity has never promoted an individualistic "me and Jesus" spirituality. Such thinking is an anomaly and an abberation. Even as early as the fourth century, when hermits started retreating into the desert to live solitary lives in radical devotion to God, the Christian tradition remained consistently adamant: love, charity and hospitality are absolutely essential, expected and required. As one desert hermit taught, the charity shown to a sick brother is worth more than a lifetime of penitential practices. Jesus said, "By this everyone will know that you are my disciples, if you have love for one another" (John 13:35). Lovers abide in God and God in them.

Born to be in relationship, the true self is also *self-giving*. The great temptation, especially for beginners in spiritual formation, is to think that spiritual growth is about the byproducts that we sometimes experience. Beginners hanker after the spiritual buzz, the feelings of peace, the sunshine of inner joy that we occasionally enjoy as gifts from God. John of the Cross calls the desire for such sensations and emotions "spiritual lust." When all is said and done, the journey of the spiritual life is a deepening in selfless love, not spiritual experiences.

The selfless quality of this self-giving is no more clearly evident than in Jesus' injunction "But I say to you that listen, Love your enemies, do good to those who hate you, bless those who curse you, pray for those who abuse you" (Luke 6:27-28). It's not about me, but about thee and Thee.

Love, indeed, is the acid test of spiritual growth. "It is love alone that counts," as Thérèse of Lisieux summed it up the day before she died. Paul reminded the Corinthians who were overflowing with spiritual gifts,

If I speak in the tongues of mortals and of angels, but do not have love, I am a noisy gong or a clanging cymbal. And if I have prophetic powers, and understand all mysteries and all knowledge, and if I have all faith, so as to remove mountains, but do not have love, I am nothing. If I give away all my possessions, and if I hand over my body so that I may boast, but do not have love, I gain nothing. (1 Corinthians 13:1-3)

For a number of years, I was the spiritual director of Mother Teresa of Calcutta's sisters in Asia. I am fortunate to have gotten to know Sr. Lucina. I still clearly remember the day when she was caring for an elderly person in the home that the sisters run in Hong Kong. I was helping her.

A wealthy potential benefactor walked in, watched what was going on and asked Sr. Lucina, "What's the point of your work? It doesn't look like much except caring for old people."

I became defensive and was just about to speak up when Sr. Lucina looked at me with a stern first-grade-teacher's glance. She simply smiled and said to the woman, "You are right. It's not much. We just take care of people one on one." And, hearing that, I realized Sr. Lucina had no need to defend a selfless act of love and charity.

Those who are at home are *unflappable and unthreatened.* They waste no time and have no emotional need to protect their reputation or justify what they are doing. They just do what they are doing, knowing full well that the Presence in the present moment validates their lives and actions.

The vast majority of us suffer from amnesia of the present. We think that the real action is somewhere else. Some of us have lost touch with the present moment because we prefer to live in the past. We are forever mulling over yesterday—regretting it, analyz-

ing it or glorifying it with nostalgia. Sentimentality, regret and guilt
are the prices we pay when we live yesterday today.

Others of us are always jumping ahead to the future: anxious
about next weekend, planning next month, wondering about next
year. With antacids in our pockets and ulcers in our stomachs, we
race toward tomorrow. Anxiety and worry are the prices we pay
when we leave the home of the present moment and try to live tomorrow today.

The late Anthony DeMello, S.J., compared our daily predica-
ment to that of a person who, at the very beginning of the symphony, suddenly realizes he has locked his keys in his car. Anxiety
divides his awareness and freezes him in a semiconscious state. He
is unable to enjoy the music unfolding before him, because his
worry has returned him to the parking lot. He is filled with regret.
He is also worried about what will happen after the concert. Who
will he call? How much will it cost? He is stuck, straddling the moment, unable to enjoy the present, unable to fix the past, unable to
hasten the future.

Contrast that man's response with a woman's in a more precari-
ous situation. One day, a woman decided to take a walk through
the jungle. While she walked along, enjoying the sounds of the
jungle, a disturbed tiger suddenly started to chase her. The woman
ran as fast as she could and found herself at the edge of a cliff.
Luckily, there was a thick vine hanging down the face of the cliff.
The woman grabbed it and started her descent. Halfway down, she
looked up and noticed two mice chewing on the vine. It was evident that her makeshift safety rope would soon give way. Looking
down, she saw a pack of hungry wolves anxious for their next
meal. The woman looked around and spied a strawberry bush
growing on the side of the cliff. Rather than regret her decision to

take a walk or worry about her impending death, she plucked a strawberry from the bush, put it in her mouth and savored the taste. "There's nothing like a fresh strawberry!" she exclaimed.

Those who have returned to where God has placed them, who live at home, are *focused on the here and now*. "There's nothing like a fresh strawberry!" they are prone to say, even in the most uncertain of circumstances. They recognize that the past and the future are mental constructs that refer to the nonexistent. There is only one reality: the Presence in the present moment: "I AM WHO I AM" (Exodus 3:14). And so, like Moses before the burning bush, they take off their shoes and develop the habit of living right here, right now.

This focus on the here and now leads to a *contemplative approach to life*. People rooted in the true self are well aware of what the Jesuit Jean-Pierre de Caussade called "the sacrament of the present moment."

Hasidic Jews believe that angels enter our lives one hundred times a day. Each day, they say, each one of us experiences one hundred messengers of God. From this Hasidic point of view, the amazing thing is not that the angel Gabriel entered Mary's life, but that Mary recognized this annunciation of God (see Luke 1:26-38). Mary was a great contemplative, intensely focused on each individual who entered her life. She looked beyond the veil of human flesh and offered hospitality to each person as a messenger of the divine. She saw Thee in thee. She was a woman totally aware that everyone she encountered was a God-bearer. The eyes of her heart were wide open, and she was wide-awake. She was living in the present, in the here and now, attuned to the Presence. From such a stance, she discovered the annunciations of daily life, the epiphany of the now, the sacrament of the present moment and the tabernacle of her neighbor.

A contemplative approach to life is constantly receptive to the visitation of angels when we least expect them and at the most inconvenient of times. One thinks of God's visit under the guise of three travelers as Abraham rested during the heat of the day (see Genesis 18:1-16). When asked by a sinner for a way to make up for lost time in the spiritual life, Eckhart said it in a curious way: "Be in all things a God-seeker and at all times a God-finder, among all kinds of people and in all kinds of circumstances."

A practical consequence of this is that if I am "looking" for God, I am not living in the here and now, where the present moment is pregnant with the Presence. And if I am not living in the here and now, then where, pray tell, am I living? After all, there is no other reality than the present moment.

This contemplative stance combined with living in the here and now gives birth to lives of *wonder and awe*. In the words of the dying priest in George Bernanos's *The Diary of a Country Priest*, "Grace is everywhere." Indeed, the true self knows only too well that "the God of all grace" (1 Peter 5:10) dallies and sometimes dances within every moment and situation. The awareness of this fact drives these people to their knees in adoration.

On a cold January afternoon, I discovered two other traits of those who have come home to the sacrament of the present moment and are rooted in the true self.

Margo lay in a hospital bed that her parents had bought and placed in the family's living room. She was only sixteen years old and was dying of Lou Gehrig's disease. What immediately struck me were the clarity of her eyes and the simplicity of her smile. A silent beauty radiated from her diseased body.

I felt very awkward and had no idea what to say. But, with a cordial sensitivity that set me at ease immediately, she faced the issue squarely and bluntly—the very issue I had been asked to discuss with her yet did not know how to broach. With a soft voice in which I could not detect any self-pity, she asked, "I guess they told you I'm dying, huh?"

I nodded my head. "Yes."

She calmly stated that the time must be getting close because she noticed her breathing was becoming more and more difficult. She explained that this muscular disease would cause her to gradually lose control of her lungs and, in the end, she would suffocate.

I was taken aback by her bluntness. I searched my mind and heart for something to say, and these are the words, I am now embarrassed to admit, that tumbled out of my mouth: "Margo, do you find it hard to die?"

"Not really," she replied instantly. "The suffering of the past year has forced me to let go of so many things—my privacy, the ability to go to the bathroom alone, the ability to feed myself and change the television channel. It seems like every day I'm challenged to let go of something else. And so, I've gotten really good at letting go and surrendering to the present moment. I suspect when death comes, it's just going to be another moment to let go and surrender. So I don't think it will be hard to die. I suspect it will come quite naturally to me."

Trustful surrender is natural for those rooted in the true self. It is born of a sense that the Presence in the present moment, as mysterious and even confusing as it might be as in the loss of a loved one, opens a pathway to deeper life. We are challenged to bow and surrender to each moment in life, knowing that the burning bush blazes so brightly at times that we might experience it as darkness. The moment we surrender, pain becomes praise. Weakness becomes strength.

This characteristic is a subtle reminder that all emotional stress and suffering in life are self-imposed. Our obsession and need to control and manipulate life, others and sometimes even God are the primary reasons we are frustrated and stressed. Those who have come home simply surrender to the mystery of the Presence. Like floating in water, they simply give themselves over to the here and now and float in the stream called daily life. Though this appears to be some form of a weak, passive resignation, it is, in fact, an active choice for trust.

A little later, Margo seemingly contradicted what she had said by adding, "You know, it's hard to die." She spoke of how deeply hurt her parents and friends would be by her death. She spent much of our time together that afternoon telling me how her death was going to be a tragedy and trial for her loved ones. "How will my parents cope?" she asked. "How will my friends be able to get on with their lives after I'm gone?" I could not help but see the irony in the situation: in the face of her own suffering and death, Margo was worried about how others would deal with the loss of her presence.

Margo was filled with *compassion,* a deep sensitivity and sharing in the sufferings of others. She could have chosen, like many do, to walk the dimly lit, lonely alley of self-absorption that leads to the dead-end of self-pity. But instead, she looked beyond "me" to thee—and, with that choice, Lou Gehrig's disease was transformed into an instrument of love. Pain became praise. Weakness became strength.

Those at home in the here and now live with an *awareness of being a spoke in the larger wheel of creation.* They know that all creatures are interrelated, forming one universal web of interdependent relationships. They live in a communion. This marvelous web of creation binds all reality together into one family and becomes a visible sign of the perfection of our common Creator, the generous love of our gracious God.

That was one of the marvelous insights of Francis of Assisi. He saw in all creation—the sun, the moon, the birds of the air and the water flowing in a stream—his brothers and sisters. However, the awareness of this familial bond with other elements of creation did not come all at once to him nor was it something that he discovered early on. On the contrary, *The Canticle of Brother Sun,* his famous hymn composed to celebrate the presence of God in his inanimate brothers and sisters in creation, was written only at the very end of his life. It was the expression of his spiritual maturity.

As part of the familial web of creation, we human beings have been given the commission by God to preserve and promote this family of creation. We are the caretakers and stewards. The business section of the morning newspaper and the evening news on television sometimes highlight controversy as ecologists and environmentalists remind us that trees serve other purposes than just producing paper. But sadly, utility often replaces childlike wonder. With air pollution, global warming and endangered species, one can only wonder if we have become the arsonists of our own planet.

An experience of mine in China highlights another characteristic of the true self.

One day, while walking alongside the Yangtze River to an outdoor market to buy some pork and Chinese vegetables, I ran into Fang Po Zhi. He was a proud, elderly Chinese scholar whose thoughts and reflections never ceased to amaze me because they were often so uncharacteristic of the Chinese. This day's encounter would be typical.

"Hey, Albert, I need your help with this!" he said. "The situation is so tense and someone must tell the West that there are other opinions here in China besides the official one put forward by my government." As with most conversations with Old Fang, as he allowed me to affectionately call him, this one seemed to have already started without my being aware. His mind was always working away and analyzing something. A familiar face often became the unknowing audience to his latest ruminations.

"*Zenma yang* [What's up]?" I asked.

Aware of the sensitivity of his latest thoughts and fearing our conversations might be overheard, Old Fang spoke in his impeccable English. "These military exercises with live ammunition that my government is sponsoring so close to the island of Taiwan are crazy! They are simply trying to intimidate the people of Taiwan and influence their presidential elections next Saturday. Actions like this cannot be justified. I must let people in the West know that there are Chinese who see the absurdity and injustice in the situation. You must give me the address of the *New York Times* so I can write a letter to the editor."

It was the week of March 18, 1996. The island of Taiwan, traditionally viewed by the Communist government of mainland China as a renegade province, was preparing for the first fully democratic presidential election in the four thousand years of Chinese history. President Lee, up for reelection, had spent the final two years of his term advocating a style of diplomacy that hinted he was in favor of Taiwan declaring itself an independent country in spite of its cultural and historical links to the mainland. Such a declaration would be totally unacceptable to the mainland government. And so, partly as an intimidation and fear tactic and partly to try to influence Taiwan's election, the mainland government had decided that some six weeks before the election was an opportune time to conduct military exercises.

Old Fang continued, "My country has been good to me. I love it. But I will never allow any form of propaganda to blind me to what I know in my heart is the truth. I want to die knowing that I stood up for what was right. So, do you have the *Times's* address?"

"I can easily get it for you in a few days," I replied. "But aren't you taking a tremendous risk? You're not really going to sign the letter, are you?" With him, such questions were superfluous, but I couldn't help but ask anyway.

Old Fang paused and looked into my eyes. He then said, "Albert, my wife is always quoting a line from the Bible that after these seventy-five years, I am just now beginning to understand: 'The truth will set you free.' Why send the letter if I don't intend on signing it?"

Old Fang hardly considered himself an unpatriotic liberal or revolutionary. Rather, he was the most patriotic of citizens, continually looking for the truth in his country's situation and willing to risk so much for the sake of witnessing to it. He was a free man who refused to be blinded by any government's agenda, including his own, or by the particular spin a situation was given by authorities who could potentially do him harm. This and other experiences with Old Fang taught me that he was undeniably grounded in the true self. Despite the consequences his actions could bring, he had discovered political freedom in what is probably the hardest place to find it, a Communist country.

Old Fang's heroic witness to the truth is a reminder that those rooted in the true self have a *passion for peace and justice*. Such people are well aware that active nonviolence can be a positive force for social change, as witnessed in the lives of Mahatma Gandhi and

Dr. Martin Luther King Jr. Love motivates their critical analysis of institutions, be it government or church, and social structures. They promote a transformation of society so that justice can be experienced by all, most especially the poor, the marginalized and those who have no voice in the world. And they believe in an equitable sharing of the world's resources.

For those who live "at home," these are not liberal political agendas. They are expressions of a Christian spiritual life that has its roots in Paul's letter to the Romans: "For the kingdom of God is not food and drink but righteousness and peace and joy in the Holy Spirit. . . . Let us then pursue what makes for peace and for mutual upbuilding" (Romans 14:17, 19).

There are moments in life when we come back to being the people God created us to be. We move beyond our self-absorption with yesterday or tomorrow and focus our attention on Thee, the Presence in the present moment. That Presence dwells within and surrounds us like the air we breathe. Such occasions, celebrations of the sacrament of the present moment, are experiences of God. Again, as Eckhart said, "God is at home."

And then, sadly, he added, "It is we who have gone out for a walk."

REFLECTION QUESTIONS

1. When am I more likely to experience the divine Presence in the present moment?

2. When am I most myself?

3. When did my life begin to be riddled with guilt (obsession with the past) or anxiety and worry (obsession with the future)?

4. How do my prayers or behavior suggest that God is "up there"

and I am "down here"? How can I better experience the reality of Emmanuel, "God with us"?

5. What am I trying to "get" in the spiritual life?

6. Which true-self characteristics are already operative in my life?

7. Which true-self characteristics are still lacking in my life?

2

THE FALSE SELF

Leaving Home

It's too easy to lose touch with who we are and become obsessed with what we are not. We become alienated from our very selves as we develop bad habits that verge on addictions. We are convinced by television commercials and become obsessed with the latest laptop computer, the newest model of an automobile and the miracle drug that will solve our weight problem, our sexual dysfunction or our struggles to have a good night's sleep. We desperately crave affection or attention and will do or say anything to obtain it. We live in the present for a fleeting moment, only to return quickly to tomorrow's worries and concerns. We become so consumed with our careers and roles that we end up defining ourselves by what we do. We are restless and weighed down with the guilt and regrets of the past.

In our journey away from the God-intended true self, an interdependent person living with the awareness of the Presence in the present moment, we have constructed a false self, which makes us forget who we really are and where we truly belong.

The false self is obsessed with "me." It expresses its concerns in our emotional fixation and investment in the superficialities of what we have, what we do and what people think of us. Our possessions, occupation and reputation absorb our time and consume our attention. Because we have been told our success or failure as individuals is based on such trifling externals, we spend our lives away from home, in a restless search to amass and accumulate whatever will increase and protect our possessions, our seniority at the office and the respect of others.

One of the opening scenes in John's Gospel speaks directly to this point. Jesus asks a simple question of two of John's disciples: "What are you looking for?" Their reply, "Rabbi . . . where are you staying?" (John 1:38) might have arisen from a very practical need. Since the Gospel mentions it was "about four o'clock in the afternoon" (verse 39), perhaps Andrew and the other disciple were looking for a place to stay to avoid violating the prohibition against travel on the Sabbath.

But typical of John's Gospel, Jesus' question can be heard on a deeper, more provocative level. Perhaps the Master is asking about the reason for their journey away from home.

THE HOLE IN THE HEART

We are born with something missing in our lives. Call it the hole in the heart. As newborns we have it, but because we have yet to develop the emotional obsession with filling it, this hole becomes the sanctuary lamp through which the light of God shines through us to others.

Very early on, however, our culture and upbringing begin to tell us not only that we need to plug this hole up but also what we should use so we can find apparent *full*-fillment. Consequently, we find ourselves climbing the fence and going on a wild-goose chase for things that we think will make us feel fulfilled. Our lives become stuffed with trifles and trinkets—a visible sign that we are not satisfied. Indeed, our stuffed lives are like the bloated stomachs of starving children. They betray our hunger, not our satisfaction.

And thus begins our obsession with what we have, what we do and what people think of us. Unfortunately, it takes us half a lifetime, usually around midlife, to discover that things found in shopping malls, places of honor and short-lived infatuations cannot fill the hole in the heart.

"What are you looking for?" Those rooted in the true self need not answer. They are aware that there is nothing to get in the spiritual life. There is nothing "out there" that can plug the hole in the heart and make them feel whole. So they remain at home, basking in the sacrament of the present moment.

THE EMPTY Ps

Those of us rooted in the false self, however, have been pulled away from where we were placed at birth and seduced into following someone else's agenda. And that someone is the false self. Because of that, we leave home and go off on a reckless escapade for personal fulfillment, turning to what I call the Empty Ps.

THE EMPTY Ps OF THE FALSE SELF	
• Pleasure	• Popularity
• Praise	• People
• Power	• Productivity
• Prestige	• Possessions
• Position	• Perfection

For some of us, the search is for *pleasure*, the emotional fix, the cheap thrill. We search for forms of diversion and entertainment. The Internet, of course, has made this a virtual journey, since we no longer need to get into the car and head to the adult bookstore, the shopping mall or the airport to catch a flight to Las Vegas. Many of us find such distractions harmless and exciting and fail to see their insidious dark side. Depending on one's personality, these distractions can easily develop into unhealthy compulsions that ultimately lead into the quicksand of full-blown addictions to alcohol, sex, drugs, romance, gambling, shopping or food.

Pleasure-worshipers have an emotional need for constant excitement and stimulation. Every day must be spectacular and upbeat. Sadly, some of us live a vicious cycle of frustration: to have a thrill fulfilled is simply to deepen our passion and yearning for it

In his great work on spiritual growth, *The Ascent of Mount Carmel*, John of the Cross addresses this issue head-on. He likens our desires and appetites to little children who are always whining to their mothers for this thing or that and are never satisfied. John notes how the task of trying to satisfy the demands of the appetites is a wearing and fatiguing undertaking. He actually compares it to digging leaking cisterns that cannot contain the water that slakes thirst.

John continues by quoting the prophet Isaiah (57:20) and comparing such people to a "stormy sea." Pleasure-seekers are not at peace. Indeed, they are incapable of resting in the present moment, or any place for that matter, because there is always a wind that sweeps them in this direction or that direction.

John of the Cross is unrelenting, stating that those who seek the satisfaction of desires are like starving people who open their mouths only to taste the air. And the very act of opening the mouth makes it dry, since air is not our proper food.

John concludes by noting how a person who seeks the fulfillment of desires is like a wearied and depressed lover who missed
the opportunity to be with his beloved on a specified day. He is
frustrated. Even if he were with the beloved, that fulfillment would
only cause more hunger and emptiness. And then, quoting what
appears to be the common knowledge of the day, John concludes
by saying that an appetite is like a fire that blazes when the wood
is thrown on it, but quickly dies out when the wood has burned.
Its satisfaction, in other words, is a bottomless pit, a whining child
screaming for more.

For some people chained to the high chair of the false self, the
whining child screams for *praise*. Some of us are incapable of truly
coming to know ourselves because we are too busy pleasing others. We yearn for their affirmation and appreciation. We are passionate about the slap on the back or the nod of approval. Our entire life revolves around the esteem, acclaim and applause offered
by others.

Though praise-seekers usually appear as happy, fun-loving people, we are actually weak, shallow people who acquiesce and capit-
ulate to the whims and dictates of others. Our opinions and actions
change like the weather. We are not our own persons. We are literally following someone else's agenda.

When my first book was published in the United States, I was
studying Chinese full time and living on the island of Taiwan. I
was a little disappointed that I did not have the experience of walking into a bookstore and seeing my book for sale.

About six months after the book's publication, I was asked to
witness the marriage of some friends in Phoenix. So I flew from
Taipei and planned to spend two weeks in Arizona. After the wedding, the bride's parents asked if there was anything that I wanted

to do or see before returning to Taiwan. "I would love to visit a Christian bookstore," was my reply. The father of the bride mentioned that a Franciscan retreat house in the suburbs had a terrific selection of books. And so off we went.

The bookstore was certainly no disappointment. It had the latest books and, on top of that, a very helpful Franciscan friar who could offer recommendations and reviews upon request. As I walked the aisles, I noticed that the books were in alphabetical order by the authors' last names. I instinctively went toward the *Hs*. And lo and behold, there it was—*Swimming in the Sun: Rediscovering the Lord's Prayer with Francis of Assisi and Thomas Merton* by Albert Haase, O.F.M. I was tickled to death. I picked up the book and headed toward the cashier. I thought I would squeeze a compliment out of the helpful Franciscan friar who managed the store.

Without telling him who I was, I said, "Excuse me, Brother. I have ten dollars to spend on a book, and I was wondering if this book would be a good investment."

The friar looked at me, grimaced, took the book from my hand and replaced it with a book by Henri Nouwen. "Sir, if you have ten dollars, here's a better investment. It's a wonderful read."

I was crestfallen. And, sad to say, those final days in the States were ruined as I nursed my bruised ego and reminded myself of Jesus' words, "For all who exalt themselves will be humbled" (Luke 14:11).

Some of us have an insatiable taste for *power, prestige* and *position*. We have to be in charge with control and mastery over our own lives, your life and everybody else's life. We have an emotional need to be king of the hill and queen for a day, seven days a week— and we will not be happy until we are. This "corporate" approach to daily living requires a title, a rank or a position that will boost what we feel we do not have internally.

Those of us who are power-hungry crave the prestige that comes with a high and important position. We aren't above becoming needy, defensive and suspicious as we protect our power base or turf. Without it, we live each day cowering like a punished puppy. With it, we bark our way through the week with endless demands. We will sometimes thrust ourselves on others, becoming aggressive, difficult and cruel.

Of course, this simply betrays a level of paranoia, the obsession to look over our shoulders, to constantly compare ourselves to others and to frequently feel threatened.

Herod is our mentor. Tragic as it sounds, he is clearly threatened by the birth of a newborn baby announced by the Magi (see Matthew 2:16-18). Unsure of the exact time of the birth, he demands the slaughter of all boys two years old or younger in the town of Bethlehem and its vicinity. Clearly he wants to wipe out any future competition that could threaten his authority and control of the people. His lust for power is as appalling as the deaths of the innocent boys.

Those of us who have bought into the false self's agenda that claims power, prestige and position can fill the hole in the heart are prone, as Herod did, to slaughter the reputation, career or potential of another. We easily victimize others for the sake of our pride, our position in the office, our need to bask alone in the prestige or publicity of the moment. We will lie, cheat and backbite to protect our little kingdoms. We are narcissistic, thinking Galileo's universe is centered on us.

Some of us leave home and go in search of *popularity*. We are the fame fanatics who run to party after party, smiling politely, telling the same joke over and over, all the while carefully constructing a friendly, likable mask. We are hard to engage in conversation because we are always looking over your shoulder and eyeballing the crowd in the room for someone more important or more interesting.

Like a Hollywood star arriving for the Oscars, we know how to posture and pose to show our best side. Sadly, behind this performance are the painful questions of insecure children: "Do you like me? Am I okay? Do you find me acceptable?" The self-esteem and self-acceptance that we lack in ourselves, we beg from others.

The lonely people of the world really and truly believe that other *people* will cure their restlessness and anxiety. A more caring spouse or one more friend, they think, will ease their dissatisfaction and unhappiness. And so begins the quixotic odyssey in search of the perfect person.

This was the great mistake of the Samaritan women, whom Jesus met at the well (see John 4:1-26). John has deliberately crafted this scene as an allegory of the exterior search for superficial trivialities that we think will cure our interior restlessness. He does this using the symbols of thirst and water. Though it is Jesus who asks for a drink to satisfy his physical thirst (see verse 7), the tables are quickly turned when the woman admits to her own thirst and continual trips to the well (see verse 15). We immediately learn that the thirst that pulls the Samaritan woman away from home and to the well is, in fact, more emotional than physical. Her thirst is loneliness, and she has tried and tried again to satisfy it with no less than five past husbands (see verses 16-18). Her trip to the well on this day might be symbolic of the dissatisfaction with her present, live-in boyfriend. The false self's lie that people can make us happy often results in short-lived infatuations and broken relationships.

So many marriages fail because one spouse expects the other "to make me happy." People cannot fill the hole in the heart, and when a person enters a relationship with that expectation, that person is doomed to experience continual frustration within oneself and anger with the other.

More than one married couple has made the tragic decision to have another child in hopes of solving the seven-year itch. Unfortunately, the child becomes a pawn between two unhappy people.

Those of us who are workaholics leave home for *productivity*. We frantically throw ourselves into activity and work, buzzing around here and there like the restless, hungry gnats that we are. We define ourselves in the effects of our labors and the dust we manage to kick up. Though always verging on exhaustion, we keep cranking out the work so that others will admire us, like us, respect us and, most of all, need us. Sometimes obsessed with a success measured by report cards, progress reports or yearly evaluations, we forget to live. Think of Martha running around, trying to prepare a meal for Jesus while her sister, Mary, revels in the present moment—the "banquet" of the Lord's presence and words (see Luke 10:38-42).

When sickness or mandatory retirement forces the Marthas of the world to stop working, they feel as if life has come to an end. Why? Because that which has given their life meaning, value and purpose has disappeared. They now feel useless and worthless. Their self-worth and self-esteem are tied up in what they do, not in who they are.

Some of us try to boost our poor self-images with the passing happiness of *possessions*. Like Imelda Marcos and her 1,220 pairs of shoes, we think that the more "stuff" we have, the more secure and attractive we are. Our self-worth is tied up in the external objects that the media claim are the measures of happiness and success: big houses, fancy cars, expensive jewelry, fashionable clothes. There is nothing wrong with these things, but some of us go after them thinking they will result in a happy, fulfilled life. Jesus' warning is well taken: "Be on your guard against all kinds of greed; for one's life does not consist in the abundance of possessions" (Luke 12:15).

The rich young man, sadly, thought just the opposite (see Mark 10:17-22). He apparently was a good man who kept the commandments. Perhaps his continued restlessness and dissatisfaction moved him to ask Jesus about eternal life. When Jesus responded, moving the discussion from legalistic obedience to challenging his greed and encouraging him to share what he owned, the man "was shocked and went away grieving, for he had many possessions" (verse 22). His astonishment and sadness clearly betray the fact that he was possessed by his possessions and trapped by the trappings of superficial success.

And finally, there are those of us who are obsessed with *perfection*. Unlike a healthy achiever who has drive, we perfectionists are driven. Uncomfortable with the fragility that comes with being human, we insist that mistakes can never be made and that the highest standards must be consistently maintained. We are alert to the imperfections, failings and weaknesses of others. Because life just doesn't cooperate with our obsession, those of us who are perfectionists often struggle with depression, anxiety, anger, frustration, loneliness and compulsiveness.

And what drives us to obsess over perfection? The desire to fill the hole in the heart with success, acceptance, love and fulfillment. But success and love rarely come to us, because the uncompromising methods we insist on and use backfire on us. Because the other person is never quite good enough or didn't get it quite right, we are deprived of the very love and acceptance we so desperately want.

Society, upbringing and friends have taught us that self-esteem comes from the trim body, the doctoral diploma, the approval of others. Happiness is having the big house, the perfect spouse, the all-American children. Love means sex or sex means love. Domination and control display self-assurance. We have been deceived into thinking that we desperately need pleasure, praise, power, prestige, position, popularity, people, productivity, possessions and perfection in order to be happy. That is an illusion. That is the lie and the agenda of the false self. And that is the root and cause of many of our sins.

CHILDHOOD DEFICIENCY

If the false self's egotistical, self-centered agenda is an illusion, a lie, and the source of our sinfulness, why do we leave home to try to fulfill it? As simplistic as it sounds, there is a psychological reason for our obsession with the Empty Ps. Often what we *think* we lacked in our childhood or, in fact, *actually* lacked, becomes the fixation in the adult. Our childhood plays a large part in setting the false self's agenda.

It's common knowledge that children raised in abusive or alcoholic families become fixated on pleasure or people's attention, affection or approval. They are prone to marry people like their parents and become stuck in unsatisfying relationships. They will do anything to please and everything to avoid conflict.

Ever hear stories of your grandparents or great-grandparents who lived during the Great Depression in America? Many children raised in those economically troubled times of the 1930s became, as adults, pack rats who never threw away anything. Their distrust for the banking system in the United States culminated in hiding money in freezers and under the bed. What they lacked in childhood, they hoarded and obsessed about in adulthood.

Paula is a middle child, now age forty. She resents the fact that her older sister's achievements get all the affirmation and her younger brother's "antics," as she describes them, get all the attention. She feels forgotten, unnoticed, like "a mistake," to use her description. And so, Paula has become a high achiever and workaholic. She runs after productivity with the hope of getting the affirmation and attention she feels she never received as the second of three children. The middle child syndrome is a common phenomenon among high achievers and people chasing after power, prestige and position.

AVOIDANCE

As the agenda of the false self gets solidified in our lives as a quest for pleasure, praise, fame, gain and possessions it also tells us that we must avoid pain, blame, criticism, disgrace and loss. And so we quickly develop skills that shun, shield, steer clear of and sidestep any form of emotional embarrassment or physical pain.

AVOIDANCE AGENDA OF THE FALSE SELF	
• Pain	• Disgrace
• Blame	• Loss
• Criticism	

There are many techniques of evasion and circumvention. Justification and outright denial can sometimes protect us from taking responsibility for our actions, while rationalization helps to promote a self-centered action that feels good. Defensiveness gives us a wall to hide behind and shields us from a prophetic word or challenge, while greed builds a wall that protects our assets and possessions. Finger pointing and shaming others can often make us feel powerful as we enlarge our personal territory and power base and as we push blame away from ourselves. Each of these, in their own way, provides wiggle room for us to slip out of any situation that might be painful, hurtful or stressful for us.

Daniel was sexually abused by an uncle around the age of seven. He has vague memories of it that continue to haunt him both in his dreams and when he tries to relax. In his thirties, he drinks heavily and is sexually promiscuous. Alcohol and sex are two ways he tries to numb the pain of the memories.

Sex, food, alcohol, drugs and gambling are sometimes not the problem; they are what we turn to *about* the problem as we try to medicate ourselves and avoid feeling an emotional pain or trauma.

The attachment to the Empty Ps and the avoidance of pain, blame and loss transform us into control freaks who are our own worst enemies. The root of so much stress and so much emotional suffering is refusing to accept what is out of our control, namely, what life is presenting us at this very moment.

The Gospel of Luke gives a rare glimpse of Jesus going through precisely this kind of emotional suffering. His agony in the garden was so tremendous "his sweat became like great drops of blood falling down on the ground" (Luke 22:44). In his final hours, Jesus was under great stress as he confronted what he apparently thought was the end of his ministry and life. He seemed to have struggled to accept and surrender to the present moment before him. The temptation was to wander from the pain and loss of the present moment and take control. "Father," he said, "if you are willing, remove this cup from me" (verse 42).

But Jesus' true self saw the betrayer's hand and added, "Not my will but yours be done" (verse 42).

The point is as obvious as it is surprising: never flee from the present moment, even if it is painful, confusing, sorrowful, distressing or heartbreaking. "Surrender to suffering as if it were a loving energy," as the twentieth-century scientist-mystic Teilhard de Chardin, S.J., is quoted as saying.

Jesus turns the me-centered values and agenda of the false self upside down and inside out. He challenges the distaste for pain, penance, disgrace and renunciation. He stresses time and time again the importance of having humility and self-sacrifice:

> If any want to become my followers, let them deny themselves and take up their cross and follow me. For those who want to save their life will lose it, and those who lose their life for my sake will find it. For what will it profit them if they gain the whole world but forfeit their life? Or what will they give in return for their life? (Matthew 16:24-26)

FLESH AND SPIRIT

Paul had his own interpretation of this. He called a life following the false self "according to the flesh" (Romans 8:5) and specified some of its characteristic actions that sound all too familiar: "fornication, impurity, licentiousness, idolatry, sorcery, enmities, strife, jealousy, anger, quarrels, dissensions, factions, envy, drunkenness, carousing, and things like these" (Galatians 5:19-21). Such are the natural consequences of a life running after pleasure, praise, fame and gain and avoiding pain, criticism, disgrace and loss.

Remaining in the Presence of the present moment—life "according to the Spirit"—results in a life characterized by qualities such as "love, joy, peace, patience, kindness, generosity, faithfulness, gentleness, self-control" (verses 22-23). The fourth-century Vulgate translation of the Bible by Jerome adds "goodness, modesty and chastity." Such a life unmasks our misguided attractions and avoidances and shows us that there is nothing to get if only we stay home in the sacrament of the present moment.

THE PARABLE OF THE PRODIGAL SON

The parable of the prodigal son (see Luke 15:11-32) can be interpreted as a parable about the seduction of the false self and the rediscovery of the true self. The younger son demands an early inheritance, leaves home and makes a new life for himself. Though we might applaud the industrious independence of the son, there is something inherently me-centered in the whole affair. But that is the nature of the false self. It feeds on itself, thrives on instant gratification, is blindly invested in the agenda of the ego and isolates a person from others.

This venture ultimately led the younger son to the pigs, a shocking image of the final destination of those who leave home to fill the hole in the heart with the attractions of the false self.

Seeing where his journey had led him, he "came to himself" (verse 17), a very accurate way to explain the return home. But indeed, that is precisely the point. The spiritual journey is a journey back to one's true self. Coming home is about leaving the pigpen of empty attractions and avoidances and coming back to the Presence in the present moment. It is about returning to where God placed me in the very beginning. And so, the younger son recognized the need for his father and became like a child again. He left the obsession with the future with which he began as well as the guilt of the past. He came back home. And in that very instance, he was born again.

The parable also suggests that the false self shackled the elder son. His anger and refusal to enter his brother's homecoming party were actually manifestations of the false self's agenda. The elder son told his father: "Listen! For all these years I have been working like a slave for you, and I have never disobeyed your command. . . . But when this son of yours came back, who has devoured your property with prostitutes, you kill the fatted calf for him!" (verses 29-30).

The elder son never felt accepted, appreciated or loved by his father. That was the real issue. He had been continually frustrated in his attempts to earn his father's approval, attention and affection. And so his resentment toward his younger brother was really pointing to a deeper issue: he felt like a forgotten orphan. His faithful workaholism had gotten him nowhere. Living in the family house, he was far from home.

"God is at home. It is we who have gone out for a walk." And so the question arises: How do we come back to the true self? How do we get back home—to being aware of and in the Presence of the present moment?

REFLECTION QUESTIONS

1. How obsessed am I over what I have, what I do and what people think of me?

2. How much emotional energy do I expend chasing after pleasure, praise, fame, gain and possessions?

3. How much emotional energy do I expend avoiding pain, blame, criticism, disgrace and loss?

4. Which of the Empty Ps do I believe I need in order to be happy? Why?

5. What did I lack in my childhood?

6. How do I avoid emotional pain in my life? (What "medications" do I use to numb the pain?)

7. When was the last time I found myself in a "pigpen"?

3

COMING BACK HOME

Breaking Free of the Pigpen

I still remember the day when Aiden, now in his late twenties, called and asked if I had time to see him. The mere fact that he wanted an appointment told me it must be something important. We planned to meet the following afternoon in my office.

He came in, sat down and instantly broached the topic. "I am so frustrated. And I am exhausted. I feel as if every day I am torn in a thousand different directions. Everyone has different needs and wishes, and I get caught up running all over God's creation to satisfy them. I just can't go on like this anymore."

"Whose issue is it, Aiden? Theirs or yours?" I asked.

He paused and stared off into the distance. I suspected I had hit the nail on the head. But had I?

"Well, it's theirs. I have a friend who is trying to sell his car, and I promised him that I would ask around to see if any of my relatives would be interested in it. My girlfriend waits for my phone call every evening and sometimes, if I get stuck at work, I can't get to a phone at the usual nine o'clock. I promised Jason that I would help him renovate his downstairs bathroom, so my weekends are spent either at the hardware store or at his home.

"So, you see, people have needs and I have to be faithful to my promises."

"Let me ask you something," I said. "Why make so many promises?"

"A Christian is supposed to be charitable and helpful" was his reply. I had the impression that he was playing up to my religious sensibilities. I also had the suspicion that his apparent focus on thee was actually rooted in "me."

"Charity is wonderful," I said. "It's downright laudable. But I wonder if you are stretching the limits and going above and beyond the call of duty. Charity is supposed to be a gift, not a grind."

"But I want people to like me," he protested.

"Aiden," I said, "you're a likable guy. You don't need to run around being the good Samaritan for every single person in order to be liked."

We continued talking for over forty-five minutes. He came to the gradual realization that he did, in fact, spend his days trying to win the attention and approval of others by being Mister Nice Guy. He also realized that it was rooted in an incident when he was nine years old: his mother, after a few drinks, had accused him of being self-centered.

"I guess you're right," he said as we concluded our discussion. "It's really a crazy way to live. I need to set some boundaries in my life. I can be likable and helpful without giving away every spare minute in my life."

Aiden was upbeat as we ended our discussion. He felt like he was in charge of his life again. His plan was to make a concerted effort not to seek the approval and attention of others. He would still be helpful but within limits.

Within three weeks, he was on the phone and wanted another appointment. When I asked him what was up, he hinted that he was back to square one and didn't know what to do.

"I'm exhausted and torn in a million different directions."

SLAVERY TO THE FALSE SELF

Ever make a well-meaning New Year's resolution that you will never go to certain Internet sites, only to find yourself, before the end of January, right back where you started? Ever make the decision not to gossip again, only to find yourself, before the end of the week, whispering about your coworker? Ever make your mind up to never again become defensive, and the next thing you know, your blood pressure goes up as you justify and rationalize some action to others? Ever resolve not to go on another mindless spending spree, only to discover at the end of the month that you've maxed out your credit card? Like Aiden, ever commit to setting boundaries in your life, only to have them crumble as you try to rein in a person whom you suspect might not notice you or like you?

Our attraction to pleasure, praise, power, prestige, position, popularity, people, productivity, possessions and perfection and our avoidance of pain, blame, criticism, disgrace and loss have backfired on us and humiliated us. Such attraction and avoidance become the chains that the false self stealthily and cunningly wraps around us in broad daylight. Think of the rich young man who was looking for more in life and yet "was shocked and went away grieving, for he had many possessions" (Mark 10:22). Think of Jesus comparing the seed that fell among the thorns to those who hear the word but "as they go on their way, they are choked by the cares and riches and pleasures of life, and their fruit does not mature" (Luke 8:14). Think of Paul's stunning admission to the church at

Rome: "I do not understand my own actions. For I do not do what I want, but I do the very thing I hate" (Romans 7:15).

Our journey away from home has led us to a pigpen where we are shackled to the false self's empty attachments and aversions. Like Aiden, we are still stuck. More than stuck, we are not free.

CALLED TO FREEDOM

One of the challenges of spiritual formation is breaking free from the conscious and unconscious hold that our attachments, passions and avoidance techniques have on us. It demands breaking the compulsion and emotional necessity to follow the agenda of the false self.

In the history of spirituality, this has traditionally been called "mortification of the appetites" and "detachment." It is death to self—dying to the false self so we can be reborn to the true self, stripping off the bogus to return to the authentic.

The goal of such detachment and death is a life freed from the albatross of being driven. We then no longer experience compulsions, obsessive needs or inordinate attractions. In effect, we can bask in the Presence of the present moment with no thought or worry that there is something else to get.

This is the "freedom of the glory of the children of God" (Romans 8:21). This is our vocation and our calling: "For freedom Christ has set us free. . . . You were called to freedom" (Galatians 5:1, 13). This is the home of those rooted in the true self: "Where the Spirit of the Lord is, there is freedom" (2 Corinthians 3:17).

INADEQUACY OF RENUNCIATION

I had been in the Franciscan Order for only four years. I can still remember the night during my theology studies when I heard a laywoman talk about her life of radical poverty. She was living on a very limited income, had a wardrobe consisting of only two dresses and spent her life working with the poor on the streets of Chicago.

I went back to the friary that night feeling guilty and depressed. Here I was, a Franciscan friar, someone who had freely vowed poverty as part of his daily life, who could spend ten or fifteen minutes in the morning trying to decide which of his many sweaters to wear that day. Guilt motivated me to look again at my understanding of poverty. I decided to give away a lot of my clothes and told my fellow friars I was opting for a simpler lifestyle.

The scavengers immediately showed up at my door and started taking shirts, sweaters and even my socks! The following day I woke up and started settling in to my poorer lifestyle. And it worked for a while. I was happy with fewer things. I didn't worry as much. I was really quite peaceful. I kept telling myself, *Now I'm living like St. Francis!* And in all humility, I took pride in that.

After about three weeks of living like a saint, however, I became frustrated and angry. I resented watching others wear my shirts and sweaters. My blood would boil every time Tom said, "Albert, I really like these pants you gave me." I quickly came to regret my decision. And before long, there I was—buying new shirts and getting my hands on some new sweaters.

Simple renunciation does not break the deep, psychological chains of slavery to the Empty *P*s. Forbidden fruit always looks sweeter than the other selections on the menu. Like whining children, the more we are told we cannot have a certain item, the more we are curious about it, the more we think about it, the more we fantasize about it and, in the end, the more we desire it.

Nor does willful renunciation break the false self's aversion to pain, blame, criticism, disgrace or loss. We still quickly eyeball the bills in our wallets before making a donation or giving a handout to someone on the street. We bite our tongues as we are criticized but secretly seethe within. We blush with embarrassment when the boss reveals our mistakes to coworkers. Though we say it doesn't bother us, we still brood and have a pity party when we discover we were not included in the invitation to the movies.

The inadequacy of renunciation and sheer willpower lies in the fact that they do not take away the deeper craving, desire and taste to blow up the balloon of the ego and run after superficial attachments, attractions and allurements. Self-centered and selfish cravings, desires and tastes are the root and source of all dissatisfaction in life; they form the womb of so much suffering; they are the life-support system of the false self. They push us out of the present moment and drive us away from home.

Holy Longing, Sacred Desire

Of their very nature, cravings, desires and tastes are sacred. They are given by God to foster the true self's characteristics of self-giving love and being in relationship. They are intended to open us up to Thee and thee and to forget "me."

A quick glance at the history of spirituality shows how desire is critical for spiritual growth. The Song of Solomon of the Hebrew Scriptures is electric with the yearning and longing of a lover for the beloved. It's no surprise that very early on, Christian apologists and mystics interpreted this ancient love poem as Christ's yearning for the soul of each believer and the soul's almost painful longing for Christ.

The fourth-century desert tradition highlights the importance of desires centered on Thee. According to one famous story, Abba Lot went to Abba Joseph and said, "Father, every day I say my prayers, I meditate and fast. I live in peace and I purify my thoughts. What else can I do to come close to God?" Abba Joseph stood up, stretched his hands to heaven, and his fingers became like ten lamps of fire. He replied, "If you will, you can become all flame."

This fire of passion blazes the trail in the spiritual life. Sometimes criticized as a heady Franciscan academician, even Bonaventure, in the prologue to his mystical work *The Soul's Journey into God,* emphasized the importance of desire for the spiritual quest. And in his famous mystical poem *The Dark Night,* John of the Cross begins by calling the fire of love's urgent longings a "sheer grace."

Cravings, desires and tastes are the raw emotions that leap out of the hole in the heart. When properly focused on their intended objects, God and others, they become the very gasoline and divine gift that lift us out of the pigpen and get us back on the road to home. They truly are a grace.

Unfortunately, for the vast majority of us, our upbringing causes us to get our wires crossed. Cravings, desires and tastes become centered on "me." They are no longer focused on Thee and thee. The grace gets hijacked and becomes a disgrace. When that happens, the journey away from home begins, and we start stuffing the hole in the heart with the Empty Ps.

INDIFFERENCE

Indifference is an effective way to break the stranglehold of the false self. It helps to rewire us and realign our desires. It makes a possessive spirit lose its craving for the Empty Ps and hinders the knee-jerk reaction of avoidance and aversion. Indifference is the malleable, surrendering disposition that allows the Presence in the present moment to shape, mold and sculpt who we are. As we read in Isaiah, "We are the clay, and you are our potter" (64:8).

Though it is one of the most effective ways to break free from the false self, indifference is also one of the most challenging keys to forge. It is not a project completed over the weekend. Trial and error based on experience hammers it out. A story paraphrased from Portia Nelson's *There's a Hole in My Sidewalk* describes the forging.

A woman was walking down the street one day and accidentally fell into a pothole in the sidewalk. She struggled to pull herself out of it.

The next time she walked down that same street, she was well aware of that pothole in the sidewalk. She was curious about it. She fell into it again, but this time it didn't take her as long to get out of it.

The third time she walked down that same street, the woman was even more aware of the pothole. However, based on her previous experience, she thought she could jump over it. She tried, but, much to her dismay, it caught her heel and she tripped.

A fourth time she walked down the same street. She approached the pothole, which still attracted her curiosity, and looked down into it. *Wow!* she said to herself, *this pothole is really deep!* Her previous experience had taught her how to avoid falling into it or even tripping over it, so she carefully and painstakingly walked around it.

Finally, the woman made the deliberate decision to walk down a different street. After all, she was now only too aware that her previous route contained a pothole in the sidewalk.

Trial and error, born of her experience, taught the woman that she needed to reroute herself. Otherwise her freedom and spontaneity would continue to be hampered as she tiptoed around that same pothole in the sidewalk a fifth, sixth or seventh time. Though the woman's decision to walk down a different street appears as brute renunciation, it is, in fact, something very different. Her decision is rooted in the heartfelt desire to walk freely and spontaneously and nourished by the harsh awareness that she is prone to falling into potholes. The woman's resolve approaches the spiritual understanding of indifference.

SINGLE-HEARTED VISION

Unfortunately, the English word *indifference* poses a problem. It connotes an unrealistic, pie-in-the-sky emotion—or perhaps I should say, lack of emotion. It suggests noninvolvement, disengagement, apathy and listlessness. That is clearly not how the spiritual tradition of Christianity understands indifference.

The Chinese translation, *bu guan xin,* better encapsulates the meaning of spiritual indifference. It literally means "no relationship to the heart." It suggests a centered heart that knows from experience what it is about and where its priorities lie. Like the woman walking down the street, it points to a person focused, involved and engaged in life's journey.

And so, spiritual indifference is really about being single-hearted. As Jesus said, "No slave can serve two masters; for a slave will either hate the one and love the other, or be devoted to the one and despise the other" (Luke 16:13). Indeed, the single-hearted and the pure of heart see God because they remain at home, focused on the sacrament of the present moment (see Matthew 5:8).

Spiritual indifference suggests a clear vision, inner freedom, committed engagement, truth and balance. It draws its nourishment from the life and teachings of Jesus.

THE TEMPTATION IN THE DESERT

Immediately after his baptism, Jesus was driven into the desert. There for forty days, according to the first three Gospels, he was tempted by the devil. Jesus, the incarnation of the true self, encounters the devil, the incarnation of the false self. This confrontation reveals an important strategy in growing in indifference to the lie and illusion of the false self's agenda.

The devil taunts Jesus, telling him to use his position as Son of God to change a stone into bread and thus satisfy his physical pleasure (see Matthew 4:3-4; Luke 4:3-4). Jesus, clearly rooted in a single-hearted truth, refuses to peer into that pothole. He retorts with the reminder that there are other ways to alleviate hunger and find pleasure than throwing one's weight around.

The devil then tries to entice Jesus with the power and possessions of the kingdoms of the world if Jesus would just worship him (see Matthew 4:8-10; Luke 4:5-8). Jesus balks at such a pathetic act to fill the devil's emptiness in exchange for the mirage of power and possessions. He clearly states that God alone should suffice. No one can serve two masters.

In a last desperate attempt to succeed, the devil goads Jesus to use his power and position for a display of his identity (see Matthew 4:5-7; Luke 4:9-12). Jesus again exhibits inner freedom and refuses to flaunt any semblance of power, prestige or position.

Jesus is invincible. He has not wandered off in search of any of the Ps. He has consistently chosen to remain home in the present moment. It is no wonder the scene comes to an end in Matthew's and Mark's Gospels with angels ministering to Jesus (see Matthew 4:11; Mark 1:13). This is a symbolic reflection of the sacrament of the here and now.

The strategy for renouncing the false self and growing in indifference to its allurements and aversions is not the sheer willpower of self-denial. Rather, we are called to learn from our experience and then return home from whence we came, like the Magi, who "left for their own country by another road" (Matthew 2:12). It means doing exactly what Jesus did, namely, deliberately staying home and standing up to and confronting the temptations of the false self.

The strength to do this lies in God's sufficient grace (see 2 Corinthians 12:9) and confronting the false self with the awareness that *things are not what they seem to be*. This is the truth that sets us free (see John 8:32) and properly orders our priorities. Single-hearted passion, fueled with the fire and grace of desires focused beyond "me," frees us and makes us indifferent to the agenda of the false self. We are engaged with God and related to the world. We make the deliberate choice to return home by walking down another street. And once home, we stay put. Indeed, the heart is now well aware that there is nothing more to get. To leave the present moment in search of anything else is to cut a path to a pigpen.

THE SERMON ON THE MOUNT

Perhaps it was a result of his forty days in the desert that Jesus chose to challenge head-on the lie of the false self in his Sermon on the Mount. He is both unwavering and unrelenting in this sermon.

The Beatitudes highlight the truth that grounds and nourishes indifference: *things are not what they seem to be*. This is the liberating insight that experience ever so gradually teaches us: external "stuff" cannot bring happiness. Possessions and pride do not obtain what people think they do: "Blessed are the poor in spirit, for theirs is the kingdom of heaven" (Matthew 5:3). Satisfied pleasures and emotional thrills cry out to be appeased again and again: "Blessed are those who mourn, for they will be comforted" (verse 4). Power is not what it seems to be: "Blessed are the meek, for they will inherit the earth" (verse 5). Avoiding the criticism and disgrace that come from standing up for what is right actually works against one's ultimate fulfillment: "Blessed are those who hunger and thirst for righteousness, for they will be filled" (verse 6). Living a duplicitous life by trying to serve two masters clouds one's vision: "Blessed are the pure in heart, for they will see God" (verse 8). Becoming aggressive and defensive is a dead-end street: "Blessed are the merciful, for they will receive mercy," "Blessed are the peacemakers, for they will be called children of God" (verses 7, 9). And finally, there is an eternal reward for surrendering to pain, blame, criticism, disgrace and loss: "Blessed are you when people revile you and persecute you and utter all kinds of evil against you falsely on my account. Rejoice and be glad, for your reward is great in heaven, for in the same way they persecuted the prophets who were before you" (verses 11-12).

Furthermore, the entire Sermon on the Mount provides a commentary on the liberating truth that things are not what they seem to be. In so doing, it offers a universal blueprint for holiness. It also points the way to the path back home to the true self.

Jesus teaches that the external prohibition against murder goes much deeper than a live-or-die decision. It gets underneath the skin and forbids the false self's anger and justification for revenge. That prohibition is intended to promote a deepening and strengthening of relationships that are characteristic of those who have come back home (see verses 21-26).

Jesus continues with the relational, unflappable, compassionate and surrendering attitudes of the true self as he raises the issue of lustful thoughts, divorce and the taking of oaths. He especially highlights the false self's need to retaliate or hate the enemy. Clearly there is something redemptive as we accept rather than avoid the pain inflicted by others (see verses 27-48).

Jesus attacks the false self's obsession to take pride, prestige, pleasure or position in showy forms of holiness. He considers such demonstrations unworthy of notice or reward (see Matthew 6:1-18). His suggested prayer is illuminating with its clear focus on the here and now: "Your kingdom come. Your will be done, on earth as it is in heaven. Give us this day our daily bread . . ." (verses 10-11).

Jesus dismantles the agenda of the false self as he challenges greed, voyeurism and duplicity. He is emphatic: "You cannot serve God and wealth" (verse 24). And then, suggesting it is a worship of wealth, he challenges those whose lives are stuck in the false self's anxiety about tomorrow's food and clothing: "So do not worry about tomorrow" (verse 34). Clearly, desires are not meant to be focused on "me."

He continues challenging any form of a self-centered lifestyle as he confronts the rash and blind judgment of others with no aware-ness of our own sinfulness (see Matthew 7:1-6). He clearly pro-claims the graciousness of God's providence and the need to stretch our horizons beyond "me" to Thee: "If you then, who are evil, know how to give good gifts to your children, how much more will your Father in heaven give good things to those who ask him!" (verse 11).

Jesus concludes his Sermon on the Mount with a true celebra-tion of the true self. He proclaims the golden rule of relationships, suggests that passing through a narrow gate is life-giving, reminds us that good trees produce good fruit and stresses the importance of doing thee-centered actions and building on rock (see verses 12-27). All in all, by the end of the Sermon on the Mount, he has totally exposed the insidious deceptions of the false self's attractions and aversions.

The Empty *P*s of the false self are not the elixirs of life. Nor is avoidance the pathway to peace and happiness. Neither our attractions nor our aversions will give us what we think they will. They are lies and illusions. They are dangerous toys that sell us into slavery and compel our passions and desires. Our emotional attachment to them throws us right out of the front door of the here and now. They are sidewalk potholes that we fall into, trip over and sometimes spend too much time investigating.

Freedom and the journey home begin with the realization and awareness that things are not what they seem to be.

ORIGINAL BLESSING

Unlike a pothole in the sidewalk, the hole in the heart is actually an original blessing. Like newborn Aiden, whom I held in my arms almost thirty years ago, the hole represents our capacity to let the divine Presence in the present moment radiate through us. It's where we belong, our home.

However, as we grow up and mature, we pick up a different message. Our upbringing and society transform the blessing into a weakness and curse. We are encouraged and taught to journey outside ourselves and go on a spending spree for stuff to fill that hole. We develop a false self whose agenda equates happiness with what we have, what we do and what people think of us. Our desires become centered on ourselves, and the hole in our heart becomes a pothole in the sidewalk.

Augustine of Hippo offers a real-life story of someone who managed to find his way back home. For some thirty years, he was caught in the trap of the Empty Ps. In his autobiography, *Confessions,* he relates how almost half his life was spent in idle and immoral pursuits. For thirty-three years, he raced after prestige and knowledge, indulged his sexual desires and even fathered an illegitimate child. He was a deeply frustrated man, desperately looking outside himself for something to get to fill the hole in the heart, to make him happy.

One day while Augustine read Scripture, the grace of God came into his life. He became aware of his slavery to the Empty Ps. Paul's letter to the Romans pointed the way home, to the true self, as it challenged Augustine to put aside the works of darkness, to live in the light of day and to "make no provision for the flesh" or its desires (Romans 13:11-14).

Augustine suddenly saw that the Empty Ps were not what they seemed to be. He saw them for what they really were: lies, poison and the chains of slavery. The words he wrote years later in *Confessions* have become a classic text in the history of Christian spirituality:

Late have I loved you, O Beauty, so ancient and so new, late have I loved you! And behold, you were within me and I was outside, and there I sought for you, and in my deformity I rushed headlong into the well-formed things that you have made. You were with me, and I was not with you. Those outer beauties held me far from you, yet if they had not been in you, they would not have existed at all. You called, and cried out to me and broke open my deafness; you shone forth upon me and you scattered my blindness: You breathed fragrance, and I drew in my breath and I now pant for you: I tasted and I hunger and thirst; you touched me, and I burned for Your peace.

Augustine had spent much of his life sleeping on the sidewalk in front of his house instead of going inside. He spent years looking outside for toys that would never bring happiness to his heart. But the moment he began the interior journey, Augustine made the great discovery: "You were within me and I was outside." There truly was nothing else to get, since he already had what he desperately wanted: the divine Presence in the present moment.

Seemingly celebrating the hole in the heart, he begins his *Confessions* with the famous declaration, "You have made us for Yourself, and our heart is restless until it rests in You." He realized that the journey home was by another route.

Augustine's witness demonstrates an important lesson. We are wasting our time if we look over the fence and beyond the horizon for something to fill the hole in the heart. Like the prodigal son, we should get out of the pigpen. We need to come back to ourselves and look within. We embrace our desires and yearnings for fulfillment and focus them on Thee. With the open hands of a newborn child and a spirit of surrender, we enter into the interior hole in the heart. And suddenly we discover it to be the birth canal to new life and the path toward home. We are born again as we experience the divine Presence, which dwells within and in which we dwell.

REFLECTION QUESTIONS

1. How and when has simple renunciation proven to be an unsuccessful tactic against the agenda of the false self in my life?

2. In what areas of my life do I need to reroute myself?

3. What would help me gain the spiritual indifference and single-hearted vision needed for such a decision?

4. How do I feel when I stare my Empty P in the face and say, "Things are not what they seem to be"?

5. How can I deepen my heart's passion for Thee and thee—God and others?

6. Which beatitudes challenge my personal agenda for happiness? How does the Sermon on the Mount expose my personal weaknesses and sins?

7. In what ways does my own spiritual journey mirror the life of Augustine of Hippo?

4

GRACED GUILT

How Our Sin Can Bring Us Home

During a spiritual direction session, Charlie once told me how he struggled with envy and lust.

"They're still considered 'deadly sins,' aren't they?" he asked.

"Yes," I said. "Why do you ask?"

"I've committed them time and time again. I keep praying for a 'road to Damascus' experience like Paul had that will change my life forever. Unfortunately, that prayer continues to go unanswered."

"A life-changing conversion experience is a luxury that only a few people have, Charlie. Most of us are like the disciples on the road to Emmaus. We struggle with our blindness and discouragement even as Jesus walks alongside of us.

"Don't look for a destination in the spiritual life," I continued. "If you do, you will constantly get discouraged by your lack of progress. Instead, treat the spiritual life as a process of awareness, as a gradual stepping into the light."

"What am I supposed to do about these sins then? I feel so guilty about them. I don't see a way out."

"Rather than stare the sin in the face and feel guilty, get beneath the sin and see where its roots are," I suggested.

"What do you mean?"

"Ask yourself: *Why* do I get jealous? What's motivating it? What psychological or emotional need does my sexual activity satisfy in me? What does it say about me? In other words, instead of treating your sinfulness and its guilt as a dead-end street, approach them as teachers who are instructing you about yourself. We can gain so much self-knowledge if we honestly listen to them.

"Guilt and sin won't give you a magical moment of conversion. But if you give them the attention they deserve, they will point you in the direction that leads into the light."

Charlie and I continued our discussion. And as we did, Charlie came to see how his envy was one way of avoiding the painful feeling of not being appreciated; his lust was an attempt at attracting the attention and apparent affection of others. By listening to his sinfulness and guilt, he once again had unmasked the agenda of the false self in his life. The path leading home was illuminated.

DIRECTIONLESS GUILT

Charlie's initial guilt-ridden response and frustration with his sinfulness are typical of many of us. Our sins pull us down into the slums of discouragement. Sins make us feel like failures, that we aren't quite up to snuff. We sometimes become depressed, angry with ourselves or at least bitterly disappointed that we didn't have the interior hardware to live up to our commitments.

Furthermore, many of us can't believe we commit the same sins over and over. *Will I ever outgrow this?* we ask ourselves. *Can't I ever move beyond this sin? What's wrong with me?* An Irish friend once described guilt to me as "the gift that keeps on giving." And indeed, it does. In its most tragic form, it becomes the spiritual swimming pool in which the scrupulous think they are doomed to drown.

Frankly, this kind of directionless guilt is just plain useless. It leads nowhere but to the false self, which thinks it's in total control of all perfection, one of the Empty *Ps*. I have no need of Thee because it's all about "me." And that breeds disillusionment, discouragement and low self-esteem. Like a dirty compact disk, this useless type of guilt simply keeps repeating what I know too well: "I don't measure up. I am a failure."

Guilt is like the dirty laundry that our sins leave behind. But our guilt doesn't have to hang out in public or make us feel embarrassed and ashamed. It can actually motivate us to get out of the pigpen! While it points to our deliberate and freely chosen actions, which we regret, guilt also has a way of pointing us toward home. It can be a wake-up call that reminds us who we are called to be. It can tell us the homework that still needs to be done. It can provide an intention and a goal.

THE GRACE OF GUILT

When used positively, guilt becomes a wonderful teacher in the spiritual life. Indeed, it becomes a grace as it did in Charlie's life. Paul reminds us, "But where sin increased, grace abounded all the more" (Romans 5:20).

The lives of some of the great Christians show us the usefulness of that kind of "guilt with direction" or "graced guilt."

Paul had acquired a zealot's hatred for all Christians. But one day while on the road to Damascus, he was knocked off his high horse, so to speak, and experienced the risen Christ. He neither forgot his past sin (see Acts 22:4; 1 Corinthians 15:9) nor let his guilt weigh him down. Rather, he learned from it in a most startling way: the persecutor of Christians became one of the most ardent proclaimers of Christ in the history of the church.

Francis of Assisi, in his early twenties, was stung by his obsession for the finer things in life and his lack of compassion for the poor. He had bought into the agenda of possessions, pleasure and self-indulgence. But rather than allow this guilt to be a brick wall against which he would bang his head for the rest of his life, Francis befriended his guilt, listened to it and discovered that his own journey home led down the path of poverty and solidarity with the lepers of his day.

Margaret of Cortona lived for many years with a man she never married. Tradition says that one day her dog appeared at her feet and led her to the dead body of her lover. Seeing the corpse, Margaret was filled with guilt and remorse over her past sin. But she chose not to hang her head in shame for the rest of her life. She saw that her guilt was pointing her in the direction of penance. And so, listening to that teacher, she eagerly adopted an ascetic lifestyle.

Martin Luther's religious perfectionism was a shackle that often displayed itself in the angst of his scrupulosity. Clearly he was under the impression that the spiritual life was all about "me" and his own efforts. He felt stuck, discouraged and hopeless. However, in his famous tower experience, he came to the realization that holiness is a gift that depends on the grace of faith. That meditation on Romans 1:17 pointed him home.

Vincent de Paul, the great seventeenth-century founder of a religious congregation and subsequent patron of charitable organizations, was renowned for his irascible temperament. He admitted that his personality could have easily become hard, rough and repulsive. But no doubt learning from the guilt of anger time and time again, he was to become a tender and affectionate man, sensitive to the needs of others.

The list could go on and on. But the point remains the same. In every case, the person listened to the guilt of sin, not to be condemned, not to be depressed but to be taught.

Guilt became like a trusted friend that compassionately showed these famous Christians where weaknesses and character defects lay. Without guilt as their teacher, these people might never have discovered the road that would lead to a homecoming party.

THE DEADLY SINS

The seven deadly sins are devastating to the spiritual life. The guilt they leave behind can paralyze us and keep us in our pigpens. But if we take an honest look at the sources and circumstances surrounding these sins in our lives—if we get beneath them and examine their roots, as I suggested to Charlie—they will often point the way back to the straight and narrow path leading home.

THE SEVEN DEADLY SINS	
• Pride	• Lust
• Envy	• Gluttony
• Anger	• Sloth
• Greed	

Pride is found in the self-service lane, where it pumps more and more hot air into an already bloated ego. It constantly seeks approval from others and yet, at the same time, doesn't respect them. Not to be confused with healthy self-esteem and gratitude for God-given talents, gifts and accomplishments, deadly pride causes us to take personal credit for everything we have, do and are, and to parade into the street shouting it. Pride is all about "me," not Thee.

Carla accidentally backed into the realization of her pride when she overheard a coworker make the comment, "Just who does Carla think she is?" Defensive and hurt at first, she came to realize that she did, in fact, have a chip on her shoulder due to a poor self-image she tried to hide. And so her pride pointed her to a need for a healthy self-love, which gradually dawned in her life as she realized her very existence was a pure gift from God. That admission turned her attention away from "me" to Thee. And with that *metanoia*—literally, "turning around"—humility was planted within her soul.

She left the pigpen with the virtue of humility. She was less threatened by others. She became more compassionate and self-giving. And she noticed a contemplative streak growing in her life as she became more and more aware of the Presence in the present moment. All these characteristics of the true self were indicative that Carla was on her way home.

Envy entices us to look across the fence and hate our neighbors because their grass is greener than ours. When we are envious, we have suddenly turned an innocent situation into a competition. We feel threatened and so covet what we think others have or are.

Envious people are prone to running up and down the staircase of comparisons: "She's prettier than I am." "I just have this, but they have all of that!" This deadly sin sometimes lies at the heart of hatred, resentment and the obsession to discredit or malign the reputation of others.

Charlie is more than aware that his envy points directly to a deep personal deficiency. He understands it as the lack of self-esteem and contentment, of feeling deeply loved and accepted by others and God. However, over time he began to reflect on an important truth, "I am who I am because this is who God created me to be," while growing in the ability to accept and celebrate the joys and accomplishments of others.

As a result, Charlie is gradually beginning to accept others for who they are and what they have. His envy is dissipating. He is now being drawn more deeply into relationships. As love and acceptance of others overcome his feelings of envy, he is feeling drawn into the homecoming party that the elder brother of the prodigal son refused to enter.

Anger is probably the most misunderstood of all the deadly sins. When we deliberately use our words, actions or silence as a weapon to hurt people's feelings or destroy their property, then we have placed ourselves in the devil's furnace of anger. This should not be confused with the just anger that is the prophet's fire that boldly stands up for what is right (see John 2:13-17). Righteous and just anger bravely confronts the individual, corporate and national evil in the world.

Sinful anger is the womb from which feelings of revenge and retaliation are born. Its manifestation is unique in each person's life. If unbridled, anger causes others to scramble; if harbored within and nursed, it can seethe and hiss like a snake filled with the venom of resentment. Often it refuses to recognize the presence and dignity of the other.

Karen is embarrassed to admit that her devil's furnace is stoked by a hodge-podge of unresolved issues from her past: the refusal to accept physical and psychological characteristics about herself; the feelings that her parents did not love her; her perception of her parents' favoritism of her younger sister, which has given rise to adult rivalry. Karen's anger is also pointed at people of other races, cultures and religions.

Sadly, Karen is still in her pigpen. She refuses to hear what others are telling her. She needs to address what's going on inside herself. Her life could be so much easier and happier, if only she would come back to herself and realize that Jesus' call to meekness in the Beatitudes gets her on the path to the here and now. But, unfortunately, like many of us, she chooses to wallow with the pigs.

Greed flourishes in capitalistic societies. It is the bottomless pit of craving more of some "thing." Fearing insecurity, greedy people desperately buy up the beach and then cling to and hoard all the sand, building what they falsely perceive is a sure foundation for the future. Greed is very different from wise stewardship or healthy frugality. It is the anxiety, hesitancy and fear of not having enough.

This deadly sin is not confined to money, though financial assets are its usual obsession. Greed's bedfellow is sometimes pride: greedy people are often ashamed to receive charity.

Greed's guilt challenges each one of us with the awareness that no matter how well we might stock our barns, we are all vulnerable and powerless in the face of God's final call home: "'You fool! This very night your life is being demanded of you. And the things you have prepared, whose will they be?' So it is with those who store up treasures for themselves but are not rich toward God" (Luke 12:20-21).

Greed calls us to the true self's characteristic of trustful surrender as we walk with the blessed assurance that God watches over each one of us and will provide for our essential needs. It also reminds us that the Christian's vocation in this world is to be an instrument and reflection of God's generosity and concern through charitable acts and almsgiving. In the end, this guilt points us to relationships and communal interdependence.

When we freely and excessively indulge in food, drink and smoking, *gluttony* is the host at the table. Contemporary science, with its study of addiction, reminds us just how dangerous this apparently innocent and fun-loving deadly sin can be. But it's not just about the heaping pile of potatoes, the beers and the cigarettes. It's about our bodies, the temple of the Holy Spirit, and how we treat them.

Just as we can be a glutton for punishment, so we can be a glutton for the daily four-mile run, the latest diet fad or mail-order cosmetics. Though we might think ourselves far from gluttony's traditional bountiful banquet, it's squeezing us tightly whenever we have a driven need or insatiable appetite for any activity, be it feast, famine, exercise or dressing up.

Gluttony's guilt has led Raymond to confront his own obsession with perfection. It led Tony to deal with his fear of intimacy. Sarah's struggle with it is a daily reminder that she lacks moderation and a balanced rhythm of life. For others like Rosie, deep-seated emotions like anger, resentment or depression have been stuffed under gluttony's menu.

Often masquerading as Cupid's arrow, *lust* is the swooning starlet of the seven deadly sins. Its slow dance begins with the raised eyebrow when something attractive or handsome walks into the room. Lust is all about "me" as it turns the other into an object of sexual pleasure with no name or history. It is the impersonal use or abuse of others for our own sheer gratification.

Lust entices us to say more with our bodies than we could ever imagine saying with our hearts. And once we've acquired a human toy or have become bored with its thrill, we throw it away like yesterday's newspaper. Lust's power lies in its ability to activate nerve endings we may have thought died in high school. Its dirty trick lies in its ability to make us violate trust and fidelity in our committed relationships.

When the pressure is on or we feel isolated from others, lust can rear its lonely head through an attraction to pornography and compulsive masturbation. Its guilt reminds us to come back home to relationships. Our flesh and sexuality are meant to be shared in mutual committed love, in integrity, respect and selflessness.

Lust's guilt challenges us to accept deeper dimensions of ourselves that we might be afraid of facing. It calls us to foster life-giving, joyful and deeply loving relationships appropriate to our commitments in life. It urges us to give ourselves permission to rest, relax and exercise in order to dissipate the pent-up energies and frustrations of everyday life.

Often confused with laziness, *sloth* is the party-pooper throwing cold water on passion and desire. Slothful people toss in the towel, abandoning all their obligations toward God, others and self. Some people willingly become sluggish, indifferent, apathetic and passive, while others restlessly flit from here to there, sometimes even in an aggressive way, with no definite purpose.

Sloth likes to sit on the porch, bored to death, ogle the passersby and dribble forth inane, pointless and sometimes cruel comments, all suggesting a weariness and dissatisfaction with the world, others and mostly oneself. It is the spirit of the living dead. It is the thick, impenetrable fog that hangs around the false self.

This sin challenged Marianne to get back in the ball game and take control of her life. It called her to develop appropriate hobbies and creative interests for use in her leisure time, to rediscover the true self's joy of self-giving. It even called her to rediscover the power of intercessory prayer for the contemporary needs of the world. Most of all, it called her to realize that life is filled with wonder and awe and should be enjoyed, not simply endured.

The guilt of any of the seven deadly sins need not be an albatross around our necks, causing us to hang our heads in shame and disgrace. Rather, it can be a lamp illuminating the way back to the true self. It can lead us back home as it strengthens the trinity of relationships between God, others and self.

CRISIS AND OPPORTUNITY

Living among the Chinese for over a decade, first in Taiwan and then in mainland China, taught me much about life. The Chinese are one of the most resilient people on earth. Despite their long history of suffering, persecution, trials and limited freedom, they have managed not just to survive but also to thrive emotionally, psychologically and spiritually.

The Chinese continually strive for their deepest aspirations and desires with an undaunted hope. Though the interpretation is debunked by western sinologists, my good Chinese friend, Ding Liang, once suggested that this resiliency might come from the way the Chinese view the trials and crises of life.

Their word for crisis, *weiji,* sums up the attitude. It consists of two Chinese characters, one suggesting "danger" or "peril," the other used in the Chinese word for "opportunity." For the Chinese, that's exactly what it's all about: every crisis, danger or peril presents another opportunity to achieve life's goal. Rather than being an occasion for discouragement or disillusionment, a crisis opens new doors never previously thought to have existed and often brings with it blessings in disguise.

We should keep this in mind as we survey our lives and our pigpens. For the sensitive and the brutally honest, such an examination can be a painful time of reflection that fuels remorse and feelings of failure. But it can also be a time when we come face-to-face with our spiritual crisis in the Chinese sense of the word. To repeat the words of Paul, "But where sin increased, grace abounded all the more" (Romans 5:20).

Our guilt reminds us to admit the sinful danger and peril we have freely chosen as we buy into the agenda of the false self. We ponder and contemplate the sources, the roots and the circumstances surrounding our sins. We may see character defects and deficiencies that we did not know exist. This deeper self-knowledge, if taken seriously, presents a new opportunity for leaving the pigpen and coming back to ourselves. This is what conversion is all about. And it's the first step toward home.

REFLECTION QUESTIONS

1. In what areas of my life do I struggle with directionless guilt?

2. How can I give direction to that guilt?

3. When has my guilt been a grace in my life?

4. Which of the seven deadly sins pose a continual struggle for me?

5. What are the seven deadly sins saying to me about character defects and personal deficiencies?

6. What are my sins saying to me about the agenda of the false self in my life?

5

PRESENT TO THE PRESENCE

How Prayer Makes Us Prayerful

What's the best way to pray?" It was a question I once asked an elderly woman who had been my spiritual director for over a year.

"Actually, the best way to pray is the way that works best for you," she replied.

"And how am I supposed to find out which way works best for me?"

"By trial and error. Try different techniques until you find one that suits you. The most important thing, Albert, is that our prayers are supposed to make us prayerful. That's the critical factor."

"What do you mean?" I asked.

"So often, people get in their prayer time and then, once it's over, totally forget God for the rest of the day. They act like they fulfilled their obligation and can now continue with the tasks ahead of them. That's a typical mistake for many of us.

"Prayer should make us prayerful. In other words, whatever we do during our time of prayer should have an effect on the way we live and act once it's over. Our prayer should make us attentive to the presence of God in the here and now—not just during our scheduled time of prayer but during the rest of the day as well. And so, as we brush our teeth, balance the checkbook or wash the dishes, we have a sense of God's presence as if God were the scent of the freshly cut roses that fills the room.

"That promotes a contemplative approach to life. We begin to live with the growing awareness that grace is everywhere, that 'right here, right now' is where the action is, because this present moment is pregnant with the divine Presence."

As we continued our conversation, my spiritual director taught me a simple technique that over the years has had a profound effect on me. I've found it helpful in developing a contemplative approach to life. It continues to challenge me to come home and become aware of God's presence in the here and now.

A Challenge to the Empty Ps

The technique is a discipline. It encourages us to remain home in the sacrament of the present moment, where we encounter God. After all, there is nothing more to get in the spiritual life. We already have what we want. We simply need to become aware of it.

I call the technique Present to the Presence. The alliteration of Ps is deliberate and serves as a subliminal challenge to the Empty Ps of the false self's agenda. Whenever we're tempted to leave home and go in search of something outside ourselves to fill the hole in the heart, we can stop ourselves at the door, remind ourselves that things are not what they seem to be and become momentarily present to the divine Presence that dwells within and in which we dwell. Done for a very short period, such as while standing in a grocery store's checkout line, or for a prolonged period of prayer, this technique strengthens sensitivity to and awareness of

God. In doing that, it helps us become prayerful.

Present to the Presence takes its inspiration from a seventeenth-century Carmelite, Brother Lawrence of the Resurrection. His prayer technique was immortalized in the eighteenth-century English explanation of his spirituality called *The Practice of the Presence of God*. Brother Lawrence encourages a person to consciously call to mind God's abiding presence. One deliberately "practices" the awareness of the divine Presence until the awareness becomes habitual and second nature. The ongoing, conscious awareness becomes an expression of prayer without ceasing (see Luke 18:11; 1 Thessalonians 5:17) as the wall separating prayer and activity comes tumbling down. The practice of the presence of God fosters a prayerful, contemplative attitude and approach to daily life.

Present to the Presence also takes its inspiration from the contemporary and popular form of prayer called centering prayer. Centering prayer has its roots in the fourteenth-century spiritual classic *The Cloud of Unknowing* and is very similar to John of the Cross's "practice of loving attentiveness." Trappist Fathers William Meninger, Thomas Keating and Basil Pennington distilled this prayer into a technique in the 1970s.

ATTENTION AND AWE

Present to the Presence requires the concentration and attention of an accountant. In other words, we deliberately focus our attention and awareness on God's abiding presence, which dwells within and in which we dwell. When we find ourselves walking away from attentiveness to the divine Presence in the present moment, we gently call ourselves back home.

To ensure that our concentration and attention do not plummet into self-absorption, Present to the Presence also requires the wonder and awe of a poet. Wonder and awe guarantee that we're focused on Thee and not "me." Without the counterbalance of concentration and attention, our wonder and awe could devolve into distractions and inattentiveness.

Present to the Presence therefore requires the apparently contradictory stances of focused attention and open-ended awe. The disposition is like the concentrated wonder of a new parent holding a firstborn, an astronomer peering into deep space or a child playing with her first puppy. When practiced selflessly, Present to the Presence engenders and enkindles the flame of adoration.

THE SACRED WORD

To express our intention to be present to God's continual and abiding presence, we choose a sacred word. The sacred word acts as a kind of road map indicating the way home when our attention wanders away from the sacrament of the present moment. It calls us back home when our concentration is distracted or when our wonder becomes fuzzy or unfocused. Thus it is chosen for its intent, not its content.

A sacred word that is heavy with meaning or that has emotionally charged significance will be a great disadvantage. Such words will entice a reflection on their meaning or an emotional response. Reflecting on or responding to the sacred word will simply lead us into a thicket of woods where we will become distracted, disoriented and maybe even lost. Present to the Presence is not about thinking or feeling. It is being lovingly attentive to Thee without thoughts or feelings from or about "me."

THE TECHNIQUE AND DISCIPLINE

Present to the Presence is as simple as it is challenging. Its simplicity catches the false self off guard. And it's precisely because of its simplicity that the false self raises objections such as "You're wasting your time," "What exactly does this prove?" or "Are you finished yet?" So the challenge lies in remaining faithfully attentive to the divine Presence as the false self desperately tries to seduce us away and pull us out of our home's front door.

Using it as a prayer technique, we begin by assuming a comfortable sitting position that will keep us alert and promote our attention. Some people find it helpful to close their eyes. Others find it helpful to focus on an external object that does not command a reflection or a response.

Once we are settled, we focus a general loving gaze toward the divine Presence in the here and now. The posture of the heart and soul are one of adoration as we open the depths of our being to discover the mystery of God, who dwells within and in whom we dwell. In other words, we collect the scattered pieces of our awareness and attention and focus them in a simple, loving gaze on God.

The sacred word helps facilitate this stance of adoration and love. Many people find *Presence, Here* or *Now* ideal sacred words since they clearly state where our loving attention is to be focused. Furthermore, their meanings do not have much meat on which to chew. Without reflecting on the sacred word's meaning, we gently introduce it as the caring nudge that brings our awareness to the sacrament of the present moment. We are not repeating the sacred word as if it were a mantra; we are not beating it as if it were a drum; we are not thinking about it or trying to arouse emotions about it. We simply use it to get us home and then, once there, we gently leave it at the door as we enter in. Once inside the present moment, our concentration and awe are riveted on God. It's all about Thee, not "me."

When we catch ourselves walking out the door and becoming

distracted, we call ourselves back home by repeating the sacred word, which serves as a road map and a reminder.

People often ask how often and how long they should practice this technique. The temptation is to turn it into the P of productivity. When that happens, we have turned it into an expression of the false self's agenda. Each of us will have our own preference for practice. Some people find it helpful to have two periods of twenty minutes each, one in the morning and one in the evening. Some dedicate an unbroken period of forty-five minutes to an hour on a daily basis. Still others practice periods throughout the day, while stopped at a red light or waiting for a bus, momentarily focusing their attention and awe on God's presence. Each one of us must find our own rhythm. What is important and most essential, as my spiritual director suggested, is that our focused time of being present to the Presence should make us prayerful during the rest of the day. In other words, we should find ourselves growing in the conscious awareness that God surrounds us like the air we breathe.

Love Beyond All Telling

This loving awareness of the heart and its holy silence comprise the technique of being present to the Presence. Two stories from the history of Christian spirituality provide real-life examples of its effectiveness and simplicity.

Jean Baptiste Marie Vianney was a remarkable nineteenth-century parish priest in the small town of Ars, France. When he first arrived in the town, he took notice of a villager who never passed the church without entering it. In the morning when he went to work and in the evening on his way home, this man left his spade and his pickaxe at the church's door and entered in.

Noticing the man never prayed with rosary beads or a prayer

book, Vianney once asked him what he said to God during his long visits in the church. The man answered, "Oh, I don't say anything to God, Monsieur le Cure. I look at God and God looks at me."

A similar incident occurred some twenty-five years later in a convent of cloistered Carmelite nuns in Lower Normandy. Shortly before she died at age twenty-four, Thérèse of Lisieux lay in the convent infirmary, unable to sleep. Her older sister, Celine, also a nun in the convent, looked in on her and asked her what she was doing.

"I am praying," Thérèse responded.

"And what are you saying to God?" her sister asked.

Thérèse replied, "I am saying nothing. I am loving him."

The heart-centered, adoring gaze of lover and beloved is the essence of being present to the Presence. And, according to John of the Cross, this silent love is the language God hears the best.

DISTRACTIONS

It's quite natural to become distracted as the false self becomes threatened by this practice and makes its selfish monkeyshines to command attention and drag us outside. Though the false self will tailor its seduction to each individual's temperament, there are five common distractions that Abbot Thomas Keating highlights in his centering prayer workshops.

DISTRACTIONS WHILE BEING PRESENT TO THE PRESENCE

- Idle daydreaming
- Emotionally charged thoughts
- "Eureka!" breakthroughs
- Self-reflection
- Interior purification

The first is *idle daydreaming*. It's quite common as we focus on the divine Presence for our imagination to grind out superficial thoughts. We suddenly remember that the clothes need to be put in the dryer, that we must make a doctor's appointment or that we still have to decide what to fix for dinner. Idle daydreaming can be indicative of almost any of the Empty Ps. However, when being present to the Presence, no thought is worth thinking. When we catch our attention and awe wandering off and following any such distraction, we simply stop, turn around and gently repeat the sacred word as a sign of our intention to return home and be present to God's abiding presence in the here and now.

Emotionally charged thoughts sometimes arise, demanding or commanding an emotional response. Because our pride might have been hurt, we suddenly feel anger or self-pity. Because our position or prestige is threatened, we might find ourselves worrying or fretting over a plan to maintain our little kingdom at the office. Sexually charged images or pleasurable thoughts might arise as we think about an attractive or handsome person. With any distraction that attempts to entice a reaction, we should not get annoyed, since that is just another thought and another distraction. Instead, we simply stop, turn around and gently repeat the sacred word as a sign of our intention to return home and revel in the sacrament of the present moment.

For some people, *"eureka!" breakthroughs* are a common distraction. Sudden insights into ourselves, creative thoughts or psychological breakthroughs pull our concentration away from Thee. Turning away from such distractions requires the utmost self-denial since we are so often attached to our own inmost thoughts and feelings. And yet, that is exactly what we are called to do. If we are afraid that we will forget the insight or idea, we can quickly write it down. That often helps us stop fussing with it and let it go. After briefly noting it on paper, we turn around and gently repeat the sacred word as a sign of our intention to return home and enjoy the embrace of our Father, who meets us exactly where we are.

One of the more clever distractions employed by the false self to command attention is focused on our pride. It is *self-reflection.* We sometimes will catch ourselves thinking, "Now I'm really making progress." Or, "this is a great feeling!" Or even, "I must remember how I got here so I can return tomorrow." Such reflections betray the fact that our attention is actually focused on "me," not Thee. It is like moving outside and peering inside through a window. It is like taking a photograph that removes us from the actual experience. When we find ourselves reflecting on "me," we simply stop, turn around and gently repeat the sacred word as a sign of our intention to return home and be present to the divine Presence.

Interior purification can be a distraction. Traumatic or disappointing memories with their accompanying anger, sorrow or fear sometimes bubble up or even smack us in the face. Deeply rooted tensions or experiences that we have repressed or suppressed sometimes rise steadily to the surface of consciousness. In many ways, this can be seen as the work of Jesus the divine physician; to use Keating's words, "the undigested psychological material of a lifetime is gradually evacuated." Because Present to the Presence can sometimes be uncomfortable, grueling or downright painful, we might be tempted to abandon the practice. But in abandoning the practice, the false self strengthens its stranglehold on us. When we find ourselves concentrating on painful memories or emotions, we simply stop, turn around and gently repeat the sacred word as a sign of our intention to return home and be attentive to the divine Presence that dwells within and in which we dwell.

SACRED SILENCE

According to the mystics, there are rare moments when our senses are momentarily suspended during prayer. These are those occasions when, as we practice being present to the presence of God, we have no thoughts or reactions. The sacred word disappears. We are beyond thinking, images and emotions. John of the Cross refers to this grace as "oblivion." The master switch is thrown, if you will, and everything seems to suddenly shut down. The tide of awe rolls in as a stunning sacred silence descends on us. We are totally and selflessly caught up in Thee. It is a feeling of hanging in midair surrounded and supported by nothing but the divine Presence.

Such exceptional moments are analogous to the unconditional, loving embrace of the father as the prodigal son returns. We are swept up into the arms of God. Such moments are pure gifts that cannot be forced or manipulated. We simply accept them in gratitude. Our very awareness of such a moment is itself an indication that the special grace has already passed. Furthermore, we do not desire its return, because that feeling of desire would be another thought, another distraction. And such a desire would turn this technique into a lust for pleasure, a P of the false self's agenda.

EXAMINATION OF CONSCIENCE

The daily examination of conscience, traditionally done in the evening, is a time-tested spiritual practice. It consists of reviewing the day's events and honestly asking ourselves where we could have responded in a more Christian manner.

A second approach to the examination of conscience consists of reviewing the actions and responses of the day and asking ourselves three questions: "What do I need to stop doing? What do I need to begin to do? What do I need to do in a more intentional way?"

Another approach to the examination of conscience asks which of the Empty *P*s raised their ugly heads today. We confront the false self head-on as we admit how we are still deluded into thinking that pleasure, praise, power, prestige, position, popularity, people, productivity, possessions and perfection will make us happy. We swallow hard and challenge our pride as we see how we manipulated and maneuvered ourselves to avoid pain, blame, criticism, disgrace and loss.

These three approaches to the examination of conscience are well worthwhile. They're part and parcel of many a Christian's spiritual practice. But there is a fourth practice that is sometimes even more helpful. It is focused on Thee, rather than "me." It is the examination of consciousness.

EXAMINATION OF CONSCIOUSNESS

With this practice, we examine our sensitivity to and awareness of God's abiding presence in the sacrament of the here and now. We look over the past twenty-four hours and ask ourselves, *When was God's presence peeking through the clouds? When did the angels enter into my day? Was I attuned to the divine Presence in that particular person? Was I attentive to God in this specific circumstance? How did God's abiding presence manifest itself to me today?*

This practice assesses our prayerfulness and our overall contemplative approach to daily living, an important characteristic of the true self. It is an excellent complement to the practice of being present to the divine Presence.

Present to the Presence acknowledges that the present moment is a sacrament of the divine. With utmost simplicity, it confronts the lie of the false self that seduces us to go on a wild-goose chase to fill the hole in the heart. This practice is a vivid reminder that there is nothing more to get in the spiritual life. We simply need to grow in the awareness of what we already have.

REFLECTION QUESTIONS

1. Are my prayer techniques making me a prayerful person? If not, what do I need to do?

2. How can I incorporate being present to the divine Presence into my daily spiritual life?

3. When am I more likely to experience the presence of God that dwells within and in which I dwell?

4. What "undigested psychological material" am I intuitively or explicitly aware of? How can I address it with a trusted friend, counselor, pastor or spiritual director?

5. As I review the past twenty-four hours, what do I need to stop doing? What do I need to begin to do? What do I need to do in a more intentional way?

6. What advantages and challenges do an examination of conscience and an examination of consciousness offer me in my personal spiritual formation?

6

PENANCE

Preserving Relationships

For most of my life, I was confused by the idea of penance. I never really understood its role or purpose in my life as a Christian. Are certain penitential practices supposed to make up for a sin I've committed? For example, if I missed church on Sunday, lied or dishonored the reputation of a coworker, am I supposed to attend a midweek church service, tell the truth the next time around or praise the coworker?

If that's the case, is it really possible to make up for that special moment of grace offered in last Sunday's communal worship? Does telling the truth the next time around actually fix yesterday's lie? Does tomorrow's praise of that maligned coworker really heal the harm caused by my gossip?

And to add to my dilemma, the Judeo-Christian tradition has continually promoted prayer, fasting and almsgiving as the three basic and fundamental forms of penance. But are they still viable and useful to twenty-first-century Christians?

When I decide to go to a midweek prayer service or spend some extra time praying, I don't see a radical change in my life—except that it makes me aware of just how holy I can act when push comes to shove.

I've never had much success with fasting. It leaves a terrible taste in my mouth, both literally and figuratively. On days when I tried to practice it, I ended up thinking more about fast food than anything spiritual.

And almsgiving? There have been times when I've surprised even myself as I reached into my pocket and gave some spare change to someone on the street. I've also donated my time and talent, on occasion, to helping others. But I would hardly look on such experiences as a penance.

I sometimes used to wonder if the three traditional forms of penance—prayer, fasting and almsgiving—were not better served by encasing them as artifacts in the museum of ancient spirituality.

What is penance? What is its purpose? And how do prayer, fasting and almsgiving—and any other form of penance we may adopt in life—bring us back to being the people God calls us to be?

LENT AND THE PASCHAL MYSTERY

Early Christians saw in the seasonal change from winter to spring a reflection of Christ's death and resurrection and their own incorporation into that Paschal Mystery. They started calling this time, which coincided with the time when new believers prepared to be baptized, by a special name, Lent, literally meaning "springtime." Those who were being instructed in the faith were preparing to throw off their old ways of life and rise to a new life through the saving waters of baptism. By the special grace of God, death would once again give way to life, just as it does in the change of seasons.

Those preparing for baptism fasted during this Lent, which originally lasted only one or two days. This fast was a way to ritualize and enter into the death of Christ, with the hopes of sharing in the resurrection: "But if we have died with Christ, we believe that we will also live with him. . . . So you also must consider yourselves dead to sin and alive to God in Christ Jesus" (Romans 6:8, 11).

Paul reminds the church at Philippi that this ritual death is much more than a specific or individual act. It is an overall attitude and mindset. Quoting an early baptismal hymn, the apostle tells the church that Jesus refused to follow the agenda of the false self and exploit his equality with God (see Philippians 2:6-11). Rather, he "emptied himself" and took "the form of a slave" (verse 7), a graphic and dynamic reversal of the false self's natural inclination and tendency. Paul exhorts his readers, "Let the same mind be in you that was in Christ Jesus" (verse 5). Emptying oneself in service of another, whether through fasting or some other specific action, was also a disposition for daily living.

Lent was gradually lengthened. The number of days was fixed at forty after the fourth century's conversion of Emperor Constantine. That number has scriptural significance. On Mount Sinai, while preparing to receive the Ten Commandments, Moses fasted for forty days and forty nights (see Exodus 34:28). Elijah walked for forty days and nights to the mountain of the Lord (see 1 Kings 19:8). Jesus fasted and prayed in the desert for forty days and nights before beginning his public ministry (see Matthew 4:2).

In the fifth century, when Christians started the practice of infant baptism, Lent was the time when public sinners showed in action their desire to repent and turn again to being the people God called them to be. Penance, initially associated with Christ's self-emptying in death, was now associated with coming home. Eventually, Lent became a special time when all Christians ritualized a symbolic death to the false self and a recommitment to the true self. This was expressed through penitential practices.

Traditionally associated with that time of preparation for Easter, the practice of penance is a way to ritually experience in our own lives the self-emptying of Christ. After all, the waters of baptism make us Christians, literally, "little Christs": "As many of you as were baptized into Christ have clothed yourselves with Christ" (Galatians 3:27). Penance is therefore an attitude and mindset that celebrates our truest identity. Insofar as we still show allegiance to the false self, it is also a form of repentance.

Depending on which of the Empty Ps we mistakenly think will make us happy, our penitential actions will be varied and different. They will not be exclusively bound to the three traditional forms of prayer, fasting and almsgiving. At times we will express this penitential attitude of self-emptying by doing something with greater deliberateness and intentionality; sometimes it will mean making a concerted effort to stop doing something; and at other times, it will mean starting to do something that we have not done in the past.

In making the practice of penance a daily and seasonal expression of our Christian discipleship, our lives get in synch with the saving action found in the Paschal Mystery of Christ's life, death and resurrection. Performing self-emptying acts of penance, whatever they might be, is one of the practical ways to come back home and express our identity as little Christs.

RESTORING HARMONY

But the practice of penance is not simply a private way to express our baptism into the death of Christ and our Christian identity. Traditionally, it has also had a strong social dimension, which has been forgotten. Indeed, it associates us with Thee while focusing on thee.

The Chinese belief in *feng shui* offers an analogy for the social dimension of penance in the life of the Christian. In Chinese culture, before someone builds a house or decorates a room, the *feng shui* expert is called in, using the words of an ancient Chinese text, "to ensure harmony in the middle."

Still very much in demand today, the *feng shui* expert is a trained, natural ecologist of sorts who ensures that a building's design or room's position does not violate the harmony and interrelationships found in a particular natural setting. By respecting the harmony of creation, a building and what goes on inside it can be positively influenced by *qi,* the powerful energy arising from the harmonious relationship between *feng* (wind) and *shui* (water), between the feminine *yin* principle and masculine *yang* principle.

If something about the building or room destroys the harmony of the setting or causes the delicate interrelationships to go askew, it is the task of the *feng shui* expert to offer suggestions for redesign, replacement or redecoration. In effect, the *feng shui* expert is the protector and healer of nature's relationships.

The idea here is not to endorse *feng shui* as a spiritual practice, but to use it as a metaphor for understanding sin and penance. Sin violates the natural harmony of the soul. It deliberately skews the God-intended trinity of relationships between God, neighbor and self that are characteristic of the true self. It slams the door of the heart in God's face. It is walking away from home and indulging our desires for the Empty Ps willy-nilly. It is ignoring our brother or manipulating our sister. Sin leads us away from home and the harmony existing between God, others and self.

That is exactly the point of Jesus' great parable of sin and repentance, the prodigal son (see Luke 15:11-32). The younger son, caught in the stranglehold of the false self, demands his inheritance early and walks away from his family and home. When he arrives in a distant country, he indulges his desires and spends his entire inheritance. All his primary relationships have been destroyed. And this poor boy wakes up one day and finds himself among the pigs, an image suggesting just how much his life and its relationships are in disarray.

But then he "came to himself" (Luke 15:17). It was as if he became the *feng shui* expert of his own soul. He started by reestablishing the relationship with himself. He spent time in self-reflection and brutal honesty. He started climbing out of the pigpen as he admitted to himself that things are not what they seem to be. That got him back on the road leading toward home, to the relationships that needed to be mended and ultimately to the reestablishment of natural harmony, symbolized in the wonderful homecoming party given by his father.

The point is obvious: when our hearts are under the domination and control of the false self, "evil intentions, murder, adultery, fornication, theft, false witness, slander" (Matthew 15:19) flow out of them. Harmony is destroyed; relationships spin out of control.

The practice of penance, as one way of imitating the saving attitude and action of Jesus' self-emptying, reestablishes the interrelationships, bonds and connections that our pride, anger, gluttony, envy, greed, sloth, lust—our attachment to the agenda of the false self—throw into confusion, disarray and disorder. It is getting back on the road toward home where we belong. It is experiencing the spiritual energy—grace—that comes with maintaining and developing healthy, balanced bonds with God, others and self. After all, the true self is relational. In short, penance does in the Christian world what the *feng shui* expert does in the Chinese world: it reestablishes and preserves the harmonious interrelationships intended by God at the moment of our conception.

SOME DO'S AND DON'TS

Penance is not some form of cosmetic surgery that simply changes the external actions of our lives. It must move each one of us beyond pushing away from the lunch table, giving some spare change to a beggar or spending an extra ten minutes in prayer. After all, we can all act holy when the curtain rises and the show begins.

Instead, penance must get underneath the skin and convert the heart from stone to flesh: "Yet even now, says the LORD, return to me with all your heart" (Joel 2:12). Penance should bring the heart back into harmony with God, neighbor and self.

That was exactly the point of Jesus' teaching about the washing of hands (see Mark 7:1-23). From his perspective, such a practice as performed by the Pharisees was an expression of cosmetic spirituality. It remained on the surface. Jesus, on the other hand, called for a cardiac spirituality that challenged the evil intentions lurking within the heart and severed the trinity of relationships between God, others and self. Those evil intentions, "fornication, theft, murder, adultery, avarice, wickedness, deceit, licentiousness, envy, slander, pride, folly" (verses 21-22), betray an allegiance and alliance with the false self. The heart, not the hands, needs to be washed.

If our acts of penance, whatever they may be, and our penitential attitude do not transform the heart, renewing and strengthening its relationships, then we might have done the right thing but neglected "the weightier matters of the law: justice and mercy and faith" (Matthew 23:23), all of which speak of the interrelated harmony intended by God. Without that harmony and those relationships, we are the walking dead. The pigpen becomes a white-washed tomb, filled with the bones of the dead and of all kinds of filth (see verse 27).

The parable of the prodigal son reminds us that penance should turn our hearts around, free us from the Empty Ps and point us home toward the interdependent relationships and obligations we have with others. Far from an individual affair between God and us, penitential practices clearly have a social dimension. Jesus makes it blatantly clear that our relationship with him is verified through our solidarity with others: "Just as you did it to one of the least of these who are members of my family, you did it to me" (Matthew 25:40).

John says it in more striking terms: "Those who say, 'I love God,' and hate their brothers or sisters, are liars" (1 John 4:20). The true self is relational.

Paul seems to have had an extraordinary sensitivity to the importance and sanctity of interpersonal bonds and relationships. He writes of "walking in love" (Romans 14:15). He reminds the churches of Rome and Corinth that it is imperative for individual believers to be sensitive and respectful of the consciences of others when it comes to eating various foods (see Romans 14; 1 Corinthians 8; 10). He enjoins the believers not to "put a stumbling block or hindrance in the way of another" (Romans 14:13). In other words, self-emptying is about thee, not "me." Suggesting a spirituality that is cardiac rather than cosmetic, he writes, "For the kingdom of God is not food and drink but righteousness and peace and joy in the Holy Spirit" (verse 17). This once again points to the relational quality of the true self.

Adopting the traditional corporeal or spiritual works of mercy as a form of penance is an explicit way of reinforcing and bolstering the God-intended bonds. The corporeal works of mercy include feeding the hungry, giving drink to the thirsty, clothing the naked, giving shelter to the homeless, visiting those in prison and burying the dead. The spiritual works of mercy consist of instructing the ignorant, counseling the doubtful, admonishing the sinner, comforting the sorrowful, forgiving offenses willingly, praying for the living and the dead and bearing wrongs patiently. Both corporeal and spiritual works promote the relational character of the true self.

Without question, penitential acts should have some kind of social manifestation or community consequences in order to be considered "Christian." They are one way of "walking in love" with others.

But Jesus makes it very clear that when doing a penance, we should not hop onto a float and parade ourselves through the streets for public viewing: "Beware of practicing your piety before others in order to be seen by them; for then you have no reward from your Father in heaven" (Matthew 6:1). He reiterates the three traditional penitential forms of almsgiving, prayer and fasting and emphasizes the fact that they should be done secretly. God will reward alms given privately. Prayers should be succinct, to the point and said behind closed doors. Fasting should never be betrayed by our outward appearance (see Matthew 6:3, 5-6, 16-18).

Indeed, an act of penance or a penitential disposition should never call explicit attention to itself. When it does, it plays right into the hand of the false self. Jesus made this point in the parable of the Pharisee and the tax collector (see Luke 18:9-14). The Pharisee was filled with pride and boasted of not being a public sinner, of fasting twice a week and of tithing his income. The tax collector, on the other hand, was deeply aware of his own sinfulness. Jesus noted that it was the tax collector who was justified in the eyes of God.

If our penitential act or attitude puts us in the honored guests' boxed seats *above* other people and not in the back balcony *among* the ordinary, if it causes us to look *down* on others and not *out* to them, then we have made a tragic mistake. We have once again been seduced into the *P* of pride.

PRAYER

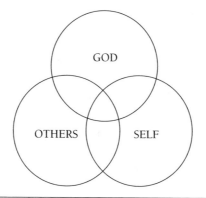

Figure 6.1. The trinity of relationships

Prayer, fasting and almsgiving have been consistently revered in the Judeo-Christian tradition as practical ways to build religious character. Their continued practice down through the ages, both as spiritual disciplines and as specific acts of penance, suggest they are still excellent, perennial vehicles for getting us on the road leading home to the true self. They reestablish and foster the trinity of relationships, the natural harmony between God, others and self.

Prayer, as a form of penance or as a spiritual discipline, is the most intimate expression of our love for God. Each of us has a different way to celebrate and express the history of God's love with us. Alice is comfortable with the rosary. James prefers repeating a prayer word slowly and meditatively. Tom enjoys daily Scripture reading. Curt is comfortable praying in tongues while his wife prays with a book of devotions. Some of us express our love for God by being present to the Presence, while others might be more attracted to solitary, prayerful walks in nature.

Whatever form it takes, prayer makes us prayerful as it heightens our awareness of the presence of God, in whom "we live and move and have our being" (Acts 17:28). It fine-tunes our spiritual antennae as we become more and more aware of Thee, not "me." As John the Baptist said of Jesus, "He must increase, but I must decrease" (John 3:30).

Our individual time of prayer not only makes us immediately aware of this graced relationship that God shares with us but should also spill out into everything we do: the care we give to preparing meals, the mood we bring home from the office, the way we relate to others, our efforts to promote peace and justice in this world. In this way, our prayer makes us also aware of the divine Presence among the hungry, thirsty, estranged, naked, sick and imprisoned (see Matthew 25:31-46). Our eyes are opened as we come to see that the man in the ditch and those on the margins of society, even though abandoned and ignored by the priest and Levite of the institutional church, are our neighbors (see Luke 10:25-37). Prayer, focused on Thee, leads us to thee. Our great challenge with adopting prayer as a penance, and thus with growing in the image of little Christs, is to *live* our prayers, not simply to *say* them.

The Judeo-Christian tradition has always held in high esteem the value and necessity of the prayer of intercession. We never go to God alone in prayer; we bring the world with its burdens and sufferings along with us. We intercede for the living and the dead because we know that the power of God's love experienced in prayer does have an effect on the hearts of others and, indeed, the world. Jesus himself reminds us that some evil spirits can be expelled only by prayer (see Mark 9:29).

One of the best ways to prepare for a moment of prayer, worship or the liturgy is to watch the evening news, read a newspaper or check breaking news online. Shame on us when our times of prayer and worship become hermetically sealed from the cries and miseries of our brothers and sisters throughout the world.

Prayer not only restores and strengthens our harmony with God and others; it can also speak volumes about our own self-awareness and self-care. It often brings us face-to-face with our sometimes chaotic and divided hearts. The growing awareness of God's presence in our lives often brings with it the awareness of just how far we have wandered away from the sacrament of the present moment, from home, from the true self. We become aware of just how restless we are or how little time we have taken for rest, relaxation and exercise. Prayer helps us rediscover and once again enter into a balanced relationship not only with God and others but also with ourselves.

FASTING

Another traditional form of penance is fasting, an ancient expression of repentance found in the Hebrew Scriptures. The house of Israel, when pressed by Samuel to turn away from their false gods and return to the Lord, expressed contrition through fasting (see 1 Samuel 7:6). When called to conversion by Jonah, the people of Nineveh called a fast (see Jonah 3:5). Fasting is a very physical way to express the fact that our relationship with God has gotten out of kilter.

The prophet Isaiah adds the communal dimensions of true fasting: "Is not this the fast that I choose: to loose the bonds of injustice, to undo the thongs of the yoke, to let the oppressed go free, and to break every yoke? Is it not to share your bread with the hungry, and bring the homeless poor into your house; when you see the naked, to cover them, and not to hide yourself from your own kin?" (58:6-7). Fasting from the injustice, oppression, greed and insensitivity of the false self are ways to restore the God-intended harmony with our neighbor.

Unlike John the Baptist and his followers, Jesus and his disciples did not fast; they ate and drank (see Matthew 11:18-19; Mark 2:18-22). In the eyes of the true self, standing with sinners on equal ground, sharing bread with them and forming a bond of solidarity with them are more important than fasting. Perhaps that is why Augustine of Hippo, repeating the ancient teaching of the fathers of the church, says that fasting is merely avarice and greed—an expression of the false self—unless we give what we would have eaten to the poor and needy. Fasting is supposed to reestablish and mend relationships with others.

Fasting, which many today think of as an individual and private penitential practice, was always intended to have strong social implications. The Oxfam Fast, in which a person is asked to skip a meal once a week and then donate the saved money to Oxfam for distribution among the 850 million hungry people of the world, along with the similar Catholic Relief Services' Operation Rice Bowl and other fasts, bring us back into relationship with our larger, global family of brothers and sisters on the earth. Fasting from television and the Internet, and sharing that time with family members and neglected friends, can help mend more immediate broken relationships. Fasting from that second beer at dinner can bring a more alert presence to family members. A most painful type of fasting involves entering a supervised program or group for chemical or drug addiction, but it can once again bring hope, healing and vitality to our personal lives. Fasting from our habits of wasting food, paper and water can help heal the very fragile relationship we have with the physical creation God has entrusted to us.

Fasting can also be a painful admission that we are prisoners of the false self, that our lives are enslaved, obsessed or addicted to external things, such as food, drink, codependent relationships, sex, television, privacy and the like. It can be a stern teacher, reminding us that we have severed the most basic of relationships, the one with ourselves, and allowed our lives to spin out of control. It can speak loudly of a life lived alone behind closed doors, of life with the pigs.

ALMSGIVING

Almsgiving is the third traditional form of penance. Derived from the Greek word for mercy, it restores to the world the harmonious order intended by God in a very practical way.

When speaking of almsgiving, the Hebrew Scriptures make clear that we share with one another and with the wider family of creation a very real interdependence. The Lord tells the Israelites that every seventh year their fields, olive orchards and vineyards are to rest and lie fallow "so that the poor of your people may eat; and what they leave the wild animals may eat" (Exodus 23:11). They were challenged to think about thee, not just "me."

In Deuteronomy, the Israelites are told that every third year they should take one tenth of their produce and store it within their towns. Then "the Levites, because they have no allotment or inheritance with you, as well as the resident aliens, the orphans, and the widows in your towns, may come and eat their fill so that the LORD your God may bless you in all the work that you undertake"

(Deuteronomy 14:29). Their charity and mercy toward immigrants and the poor help foster and strengthen the Israelites' relationship with the Lord. Harmony with God comes through establishing harmony with the neighbor. To quote John again, "Those who say, 'I love God,' and hate their brothers or sisters, are liars" (1 John 4:20).

But almsgiving is more than the simple charity and philanthropy that is expressive of a merciful, compassionate heart. For the harmonious, God-intended order—what Paul calls "a fair balance" (2 Corinthians 8:14)—to be reestablished, we must be aware of what the great Almsgiver has given to each one of us in Christ. Remembering Thee brings us to thee. And so it begins with an awareness of and appreciation for God's relationship with us.

It was because of the spiritual blessings Christ had given to the Gentiles that Paul could then encourage them to share their material blessings with the poor of Jerusalem (see Romans 15:25-27; 1 Corinthians 16:1-3). We Christians give alms to the poor and needy as an acknowledgement and expression of gratitude for what we have been given by God in Christ.

Christian almsgiving challenges each one of us to stretch the size of our hearts so that the lives of others are enriched, following the example of Christ, whom Paul proposes as *the* model of almsgiving: "For you know the generous act of our Lord Jesus Christ, that though he was rich, yet for your sakes he became poor, so that by his poverty you might become rich" (2 Corinthians 8:9). In his self-emptying, Christ was saying explicitly, "It's all about thee, not 'me.'"

Furthermore, following the example of the poor widow whose generous gift captured Jesus' attention, we give from our poverty and not merely from our abundance (see Mark 12:41-44). Almsgiving is a challenge if we have bought into the agenda of the false self that craves possessions and desperately tries to avoid loss.

We express this traditional form of penance by sharing our time, talents and treasures. Bill gives the clothes he no longer wears to a homeless shelter. Mary Jo writes out a generous check to a charitable organization. Therese donates time to a soup kitchen in thanksgiving for the Bread of Life, while Jeff writes a note of encouragement to someone preparing for baptism at his church. Mike shares the water of the world and its effect in his own life by washing his dishes by hand instead of doing a small load in the dishwasher; he also makes a point of turning the faucet off while brushing his teeth. All of us can share other resources of the earth through voluntary recycling. Carmen baby-sits without pay for some busy parents she knows whose schedules do not afford them the luxury of a night on the town. And when we give unconditional forgiveness to someone who has hurt us deeply, we offer the most precious of alms. When all is said and done, the important thing is not *how much* we give of our time, talents or treasures but *that* we give and share with those who are less fortunate. In doing that, harmony returns, the trinity of relationships is strengthened, and a "fair balance" is reestablished.

COMING HOME

Penance should bring us back home to the sacrament of the present moment, where our relationships with God, others and self are rooted and flourish. It should deepen our awareness and experience of God, who goes out of the way to greet us with open arms in every moment of life, like the father of the prodigal son. In imitation of the self-emptying of Christ, prayer, fasting, almsgiving and our daily penitential disposition open up the door of the heart as we roll out the red carpet for our brothers and sisters who are in need of forgiveness, companionship, encouragement and the basic essentials of life. It's all about thee, not "me."

All of this lays the foundation for God's intended harmony and Paul's fair balance. It also strengthens a sense of our identity as little Christs and challenges us to think about our unique roles in God's plan for creation.

REFLECTION QUESTIONS

1. How do I express my identity as a little Christ and empty myself?

2. How have my penitential practices moved beyond cosmetic spirituality to cardiac spirituality?

3. Are my penitential practices authentically Christian?

4. How do my penitential practices strengthen and promote the trinity of relationships between God, others and self?

5. How does the agenda of the false self affect or influence my prayer, fasting and almsgiving?

6. How do I know if my prayer, fasting and almsgiving are leading me home to the sacrament of the present moment and the true self?

7

DISCERNMENT

Becoming a Dream Keeper

Aiden had been dating Melissa for over four years. They talked on the phone every night. They spent many weekends together. I just presumed their engagement was a done deal.

Then Aiden surprised me with a question: "How do you know if it's God's will that you marry someone?"

Before I could reply to his question, he continued, "I love Melissa. We get along fine. We've gotten to know a lot about each other. I can easily see myself spending the rest of my life with her and growing old together. But how do I know if she's the one God has picked out for me?"

I was taken aback by Aiden's suggestion that God might have a master blueprint or predetermined script for his life that he was challenged to figure out and hopefully "get right." That sounded to me like the pagan notion of fate. After all, don't we have free will? Don't we shape the direction of our lives?

And if, in fact, we do have the freedom to shape our lives, it's all the more imperative that we break the stranglehold of the false self and become again the people God intends for us to be. After all, we are not our own; we have been bought with a price (see 1 Corinthians 6:19).

FREE WILL

Our free will is one of the most precious gifts God has given to us. It gives us the freedom to make deliberate personal choices and so shape the quality of our lives. Gift that it is, free will is never violated by God.

God certainly desires human free will to play a role in the great dream for creation called salvation history. Indeed, we cannot read the story of Mary's and Joseph's annunciations (see Matthew 1:18-25; Luke 1:26-38) without being moved by God's humility in asking for help. Never to impose, God seeks to inspire collaborators in making the divine dream a reality. As Paul writes, "We are God's servants, working together" (1 Corinthians 3:9).

Christian decision making, traditionally called discernment, must free us to participate dynamically, creatively and uniquely in the process of salvation history. It must also help illumine those areas of our lives that continue to cater to the agenda of the false self and that point to the path toward home. With great humility, God continues to seek free servants who will make the divine dream come true.

THE HEAD, THE HEART AND THE GUT

Discernment has a lot to do with making a good decision. And good decisions demand listening to the head, the heart and the gut.

The process of discernment does not abandon intelligence, good judgment or common sense. Some decisions just stand out and make plain old good sense. Yet discernment is not simply an intellectual affair.

Discernment also gives attention to desires, affections and the deepest yearnings of the heart. John of the Cross reminds us in the commentary to his *Spiritual Canticle* that God communicates to us precisely through the attractions of the heart. What we experience as a deep desire could very well be the invitation of God. This, of course, can be tricky since the heart is sometimes in the clutches of the false self. That provides all the more reason to confront its agenda with the realization that things are not what they seem to be and to return home. It is at home in the present moment that the true self celebrates its harmonious relationships with God, others and self. To ignore what the true self wants or desires in a particular situation violates personal integrity; it also threatens one way that God communicates divine hopes and dreams to us.

Finally, discernment listens to intuition and insight—our gut. Our bodies provide a wealth of experience-based wisdom in their physical reactions to various choices. Ignatius of Loyola, the great master of discernment, writes of *sentir,* the felt knowledge of the body. He calls the positive feelings of peace, joy, hope and confidence "consolations" and indicates they point home to the true self. He calls the negative feelings of doubt, fear, anxiety and discouragement "desolations" and indicates they point to the false self's pigpen. A decision might make all the sense in the world but still not "feel right." And so, good decisions follow the time-tested advice: "Trust your feelings, but use your head."

Sometimes a person, as Aiden seemed to hint, will describe the attraction to a particular decision, saying, "That's what I want. But I don't know what God wants." Indeed, there is an assumption that God's will has to be different from our own.

Of course, discernment of the will of God cannot be reduced simply to our whims, wishes and wants. However, it does not necessarily lie in what is diametrically opposed to where our head, heart and gut point. As the Latin root of *discernere* suggests, it demands the knack of "separating off," "distinguishing," and "sifting away." And that which has to be separated, distinguished and sifted are the allegiance, alliance and acceptance of the false self's agenda. Once disengaged from the pigpen, we find ourselves on the way home to where God intends us to be. We can then authentically discern what is the best decision to make.

DECISION MAKING AND DISCERNMENT

There are four components that have shaped and made us the persons we are today. The head, heart and gut must listen to them as we begin the process of making a good decision.

Past history. Our upbringing, the values which we were taught and which we assimilated, the deficiencies of our family lives and their psychological effects on us and our education have all played a role in bringing us to this present moment of decision making. Added to that are our responses to past situations and the consequences that resulted. The elements of our past usually have a limiting, though not necessarily crippling, effect on the present.

If a person only had an elementary school education, for example, he or she has to take an honest look at the desire to become a lawyer or a college professor. The lack of higher education does not mean the person is incapable of going back to school or lacks the intellectual abilities to fulfill that dream. It simply means that the past might narrow the person's possibilities or options.

Potential. As the past tends to limit us, our talents and abilities open up possibilities. These God-given personal gifts make us diamonds in the rough. Talents and abilities are the keys that help unlock the future. They can allow an adult who only had an elementary school education to become a lawyer or a college professor. In any important moment of decision, there is always a tension between the past and our potential. The past might stack the deck against us, but our talents and abilities are wild cards in the game of life.

Present identity. Our past and potential come together in our present identity, with its commitments and responsibilities. Our present commitment to others in marriage, in the single life or in a vowed religious community as well as the responsibilities that such commitments place on us need to be respected. This requires dialogue with the significant people in our present situation. We cannot simply step away from the present to walk into the future. When we do, we're walking away from home. The future is a bud of the present moment and blossoms in it. It is not a stem grafted onto it.

Hopes, dreams and desires. Sometimes unconscious, our hopes and dreams are the gasoline of life. Hopes and dreams give us ambition, energy and meaning. Desires fuel vitality and passion and provide us with deep, enduring motivation. We run the risk of feeling detached, apathetic and uninvolved in our choice if the decision-making process ignores this trinity.

Hopes, dreams and desires bridge the chasm that doubts and fears dig between the present and the future. They give us the courage to take a risk, to try walking on water, to surrender in faith when the false self tells us to avoid possible pain, blame, disgrace or loss.

Thomas Merton used to ask the young novices of the Abbey of Gethsemani two important questions: "What do you really want out of life?" and "What's stopping you from getting it?" These two questions can help make explicit our motivating dreams and desires. They encourage us to come to grips with the potential of the present moment. They also challenge us to confront the fears, doubts and obstacles that the false self throws at us to frighten and frustrate us.

Authentic hopes, dreams and deep, recurrent desires can also manifest themselves in our fantasies and daydreams. A good exercise is to allow a fantasy or daydream to play out in our heads. This is what Aiden must have done, which prompted him to say, "I can easily see myself spending the rest of my life with Melissa and growing old together." Once the fantasy or daydream has come to an end, we ask ourselves if we feel bored, empty and disconnected, suggesting the enticement of the false self, or hopeful, encouraged and in relationship, suggesting the true self. Fantasies and daydreams have a wisdom all their own.

INDIFFERENCE

A decision naturally surfaces as the head, heart and gut consider, contemplate and listen to our past, our potential, our present identity and our hopes, dreams and desires. If it is a knee-jerk reaction based on the attraction to the Empty *P*s or on the avoidance of blame, pain, disgrace and loss, we are in all probability choosing a direction away from home and away from the person God intends us to be. Furthermore, a strongly felt surge of initial resistance to one particular option may be an indicator not that this would be an unwise or poor decision but, more fundamentally, that some aspect of the false self's agenda is being threatened or attacked.

Good decisions blossom in the sacrament of the present moment. They require that indifference—*bu guan xin,* "no relationship to the heart"—that washes over us as we confront the agenda of the false self with the realization that things are not what they seem to be. Far from apathy, complacency or disinterest, this indifference shows a heart that is focused and engaged. It also is an expression of inner freedom, openness and balance.

Pete had been a Franciscan friar for six years. He was not really happy. But he was not unhappy either. He just assumed that his emotionless approach to life was part of his introverted personality.

Pete was making a thirty-day retreat in preparation for his final profession of lifelong vows to the Franciscan lifestyle. What started out as an innocent question asked by his retreat director provoked a startling revelation. The question: "What do *you* really want?"

Pete felt truly secure and confident about his ministerial plans to work with Hispanics. They capitalized on his ability to learn another language and be comfortable in another culture. But being a Franciscan was another matter. Something clicked inside Pete as soon as he allowed himself to be objective enough to reflect on his motivations for being a Franciscan friar. His Franciscan vocation was more a product of parental pressure than of personal desire. During the next five days, Pete's heart became restless as he realized more and more that, committed to his Christian faith though he was, Franciscan life was not where he belonged.

Once he crossed that bridge and gave himself permission to ask himself what *he* wanted, Pete came alive emotionally for the first time that he could remember. His heart was set free, and he started feeling emotions: relief, happiness, inner peace. These consolations were indications that he was on his way home.

Freed from the desire to please his parents, Pete was in a position to make his own decision about the future. Today he is happily married and doing ministry in a Spanish-speaking church.

Made with the indifference that provides inner freedom, openness and balance, such good decisions provide a deeper sense of our truest identity. They are homecoming celebrations. And when a fifth component is included for consideration and contemplation, the decision-making process is transformed into the discernment of God's will.

THE DREAM OF GOD

No sooner did I get back to the United States from eleven and a half years as a missionary in mainland China than I got a phone call from my nephew, Ryan, and his wife, Yvonne. They were ecstatic. Miles Conrad Haase had just been born.

"Uncle Albert, you just won't believe it. He's such a gorgeous baby. And every time I look at his hands, I just can't believe how strong they look. I guarantee you: little Miles is going to be the first quarterback to bring the New Orleans Saints to the Super Bowl!"

As I laughed, I became aware again that all parents have hopes and dreams for their children. God too had a dream for creation. The very fact that the Garden of Eden was a paradise hints at God's dream. All creation was interrelated and interdependent like an intricate spider's web. God's presence was so immediate that God could be heard walking in the garden at the time of the evening breeze (see Genesis 3:8). Indeed, creation was "very good" (1:31).

Divine attention riveted on Adam and Eve. The heart of God, like that of any other captivated parent, began brimming over with hopes and wishes. God so loved and marveled at Adam and Eve that God gave them the greatest gift possible. God placed all creation into their laps and made them its stewards. They were to nurture this world with tender care, all the while preserving it as a place where there would be no war, violence or distrust; a place where there would be no racism, inequality or prejudice; and a place where the hearts of creation's family would reach out to one another. Adam and Eve were given free will and became the stewards of God's dream for peaceful, just and loving relationships.

ORIGINAL SIN

But God's dream was soon transformed into a nightmare. Adam and Eve, by freely choosing to ignore this dream, committed the original sin. The false self appeared like lightning, easing God out and pretending to be the lord of creation.

With the entry of this stranger and intruder, creation was thrown into disarray and knocked out of balance. The intricate web of relationships was destroyed as bonds and connections were severed. By failing to preserve the dream, Adam and Eve also lost the immediate awareness of God's all-embracing presence in the present moment; it would now have to be "practiced." And God's paradise became a fuzzy memory as Adam and Eve were driven from their home (see Genesis 3:24).

God then sent the prophets to remind the chosen people of the dream. The prophets emphasized time and time again the relationships and interdependence that are characteristic of God's dream. The dream included a world of peace, where swords would be beaten into plowshares and spears into pruning hooks. The dream included a world of justice, where the widow and orphan would have their fair share. The dream included a world of love, where the stranger and pilgrim would be welcomed and offered hospitality.

THE KINGDOM OF GOD

Expressing the depths of divine love, God sent Jesus. Jesus called the dream the "kingdom of God" and in twenty-nine Gospel stories and comparisons taught its essentials about peace, justice and love. The earliest Gospel begins with Jesus' proclamation: "The time is fulfilled, and the kingdom of God has come near" (Mark 1:14). Indeed, he was the enfleshment of God's dream.

Jesus befriended the social and religious outcasts of his day (see Matthew 11:19; Luke 15:1). At the synagogue of Nazareth, he proclaimed his commitment to peace and justice (see Luke 4:16-21). He challenged his listeners to mend broken relationships with forgiveness and to love their enemies (see Matthew 6:12, 14-15; 5:43-48). Jesus told parables, urging his listeners to return home (see Luke 15:11-32) and let the kingdom come into their lives (see Matthew 13:1-58). In his self-emptying life, death and resurrection, Jesus healed the broken relationships in the world and showed his followers how to do the same. Indeed, he invited his followers to play a role in the history of salvation.

COMPONENTS OF DISCERNMENT

- A person's past history
- A person's potential
- A person's present identity
- A person's hopes, dreams and desires
- A person's baptismal commitment

THE BAPTISMAL RESPONSE

I once met a priest who had spent time studying some primitive tribes in Kenya. He told me that one particular tribe had an almost mystical connection to the primal element of fire. During their long rainy season, certain elders of the tribe were designated as keepers of the flame. Through the driving afternoon rains, these elders had the responsibility of preserving a fire in their huts. Losing the fire was tantamount to losing the heart of the tribe.

In a similar way, a Christian is called to be a keeper of the dream.

One's baptismal incorporation into the life, death and resurrection of Jesus—we are little Christs—is a public commitment to keep the dream alive; to empty ourselves and mend the bonds and relationships broken by the false self; to build God's kingdom of peace, justice and love; to come home to what we already have and who we really are, the true self.

Hence, this *baptismal commitment* should affect and inform every process of making a decision. This is the crucial fifth component that transforms the decision-making process into the Christian discernment of the will of God. As an expression of our Christian discipleship, the decision-making process seriously incorporates the following questions: How can I uniquely contribute to God's kingdom in this situation? How can I best make God's dream a reality here and now? How can I foster the kingdom's peace, justice and love? Which option best helps to manifest these kingdom characteristics?

GIFT TO GOD

God's will is not some predetermined, preordained decision from on high that we must struggle to figure out and then buckle under to obey. That seemed to be Aiden's belief in asking if Melissa was "the one" God had picked out for him.

Rather, we are left to freely shape the gift of life that God has given us in light of the original dream for all creation. Through our upbringing, talents, abilities and deepest desires, God presents us with canvas, paint and brushes. We become the artists of our own lives. Discerning God's will is nothing more than responding to a situation with our unique, gifted contribution to God's dream for creation. We make the choice to respond to God's humble invitation to be a servant and play a role in the history of salvation. And so the portrait of our lives becomes our gift back to God.

When we make major decisions in light of our unique contributions to the kingdom of God, we become dream keepers. This is what it means to be a little Christ, to do our part in building the kingdom and sharing God's dream with all we encounter.

Authentic Christian discernment is never a private, individual process. Though it demands a radical freedom from the false self and an honest self-knowledge, it is always done in a communal setting: with family and friends, those affected by our decision and our spiritual director in dialogue with the Scriptures and the church. We should beware and be suspicious of any discernment process made privately or that needs to be kept secret. Refusal to dialogue, fear of community and contentment in darkness are indications that the chaff of the false self has not been sifted.

CATCHING THE DREAM

I arrived for my first visit to the Grand Canyon rather late in the evening. It was already dark. But my curiosity and excitement at seeing the canyon would not keep until morning. So I went to the southern rim to take a look. All I saw through the darkness was a big hole. No splendor, no majesty. I went back to my motel, decided that my disappointment was not going to ruin this vacation and fell asleep.

The following morning I got up before dawn. For years I had heard about the miracle of sunrise over the Grand Canyon. So I started back to the rim, careful not to let my excitement or anticipation get the better of me. As the morning sun inched its way into the sky and offered light to the earth, the big hole suddenly started coming alive with shades of red, purple, blue and yellow. It was the same old canyon as the night before, but in the light of the morning sun, everything looked so different.

Likewise, the more we consciously take steps toward home and the present moment, the more we find ourselves moving out of the shadows and into the light. We begin to see the part that we can uniquely play in helping establish God's kingdom and making the dream a reality. It will be the same old me but, seen in the light of my baptismal commitment to the dream, it will seem so different. Our actions and attitudes will take on a deeper meaning and significance.

Some of our commitments and obligations might have to change. That happens not because of infidelity, but precisely because of the deepening appreciation for and fidelity to our baptism and our maturing responsibility and free response to the dream of the kingdom. It's not a question of what God wants of me. It's a question of what I want to give to God.

Kathy is an exceptionally bright, articulate lawyer. After graduating from the University of Chicago, she started working for a large and prestigious law firm. Within five years she had climbed the ladder of success. During those years, however, she also began to see and experience the harsh injustices of the American legal system. "Basically, only the rich can afford to have justice served," she told me at our first spiritual direction session.

After much prayer and a weekend retreat, Kathy decided that she risked losing her faith in God and the system of law if she did not make a change. So she went into private practice and started doing advocacy work for a number of humanitarian agencies.

But that wasn't the end of Kathy's discernment process. Successful as she has been in private practice, she continues to respond to God's grace and to remain home in the sacrament of the present moment. She has now temporarily given up the law practice and begun graduate studies in Christian ethics. Her dream is to teach future lawyers how to bring together the practice of law with the teachings of the gospel.

In 1988, the movie *Tucker: The Man and His Dream* was released. The film is based on the true-life story of Preston Tucker, a grandiose schemer who had the dream to produce the best cars ever made. Shortly after World War II, with the assistance of Abe Karatz and some impressive salesmanship on his part, Tucker obtained funding and began to build his factory.

At one point in the movie, two of Tucker's friends are gossiping about him. One friend turns to the other and says, "Don't get close to him! You might catch his dream!"

Catching the dream—that's the goal of spiritual formation. The more we catch the dream, the closer we are to home and to being who God intends us to be. And in catching God's dream, our will comes into communion with the will of God.

This communion is not slavery. Catching the dream triggers a deep transformation that frees our whole being—the head, heart and gut—from bondage to the false self. This interior transformation becomes evident in how we live. We adopt a self-emptying lifestyle that increasingly gives witness to the kingdom characteristics of peace, justice and love. This transformation is the greatest glory of humanity and reveals our identity as little Christs.

REFLECTION QUESTIONS

1. What does the expression "the will of God" mean to me?

2. In making a good decision, which do I tend to rely on the most—my head, my heart or my gut? On which do I rely on the least?

3. How do I express my vocation as a dream keeper?

4. How do the kingdom of God and its characteristics play a role in the decisions I make?

5. How is my will coming into communion with the will of God?

8

THE SPIRITUAL DIRECTOR

A Companion on the Journey Home

Coming home to the true self is a lifelong, challenging task. Just when we think we're growing in our identity as little Christs, we find ourselves back in the pigpen, attached to the Empty Ps and desperately trying to avoid pain, blame, criticism, disgrace and loss. Because this struggle can be discouraging, we might be tempted to abandon our spiritual formation. It's helpful, at times, to seek encouragement and direction.

Added to that, it can be advantageous to talk with someone about our struggles with sinfulness and guilt. Once we lay our embarrassment aside, a listening ear can sometimes help us discern and name our motivations. That can be helpful in transforming our sins and guilt into spiritual teachers.

As we commit to a daily and seasonal practice of prayer and penance, we might have spiritual experiences that leave us confused or puzzled. Furthermore, as we try to discern what we want to give to God, we will most certainly encounter times when we need input from others.

Upon returning to the United States after my years in mainland China, I heard that one of our Franciscan friars was in need of a kidney transplant. After some prayer and reflection, I decided to offer one of mine if I proved to be a match. However, in a very challenging talk with my spiritual director, I came to realize that laudatory though my offer might appear, it was, in fact, all about "me" and rooted in the agenda of the false self. I would never have come to that realization had it not been for my spiritual director.

All of this betrays Jesus' good sense in sending disciples out on mission two by two rather than alone (see Mark 6:7). It highlights Nicodemus's need in seeking out Jesus and asking how to be reborn after becoming an adult (see John 3:1-21). It gives an insight into the two disciples who walked toward Emmaus and discussed their deflated hopes with one another (see Luke 24:13-35). Indeed, there is wisdom in having a companion on the journey home.

AN ANCIENT TRADITION

Over eighteen centuries ago, in the deserts of Egypt, Palestine and Syria, Christians who took an acute interest in the spiritual life started seeking out elders for spiritual advice and help in staying faithful to the journey home. This practice continued two centuries later in Ireland. By the sixteenth century, Ignatius of Loyola and his followers were offering spiritual exercises to awaken people to their slavery to what I've called the Empty Ps and to help them discern their unique contribution to God's dream for creation. Today, in the twenty-first century, many Christians from all walks of life have a spiritual director.

Carolyn, a single mother of two children, finds spiritual direction helpful for making herself attentive to the wonder of God's creation in her job as a veterinarian. Bill, a lawyer, attributes his openness to an unusually large number of *pro bono* cases to what he has discovered in his two years of spiritual direction. Margaret, a cafeteria worker in a high school, enjoys the opportunity to discuss spiritual topics that are of no interest to her husband. Ordinary people who are serious about spiritual formation seek out the time-honored practice of spiritual direction to help them come back to the sacrament of the present moment.

What exactly is spiritual direction? What do we "do"? How do we get started?

A MISNOMER

Tim, a twenty-five-year-old, non-churchgoing Christian, arrived for his first spiritual direction appointment with me. After the initial introduction and pleasantries, he began, "So, Father, what am I supposed to do to get my faith back?"

There was an awkward pause as he obviously waited for me to give him the key that unlocks the door of doubts.

Just about any seasoned spiritual director will tell us that the name "spiritual direction" is imprecise. Some refer to it as "spiritual advising," and that too is inaccurate. Both names imply, as Tim assumed, a teacher-student relationship in which the teacher, the director, instructs the student, the directee. It suggests taking notes, learning techniques and maybe even bending to another's opinion or will. Worse, it implies that the director knows exactly how God acts in every person's life and that the directee's task is simply to accept the director's perspective and point of view.

Though there may be the occasional session when a director offers invitations and advice culled from his or her own experience, the primary focus is clearly not on the director but on the directee. As the directee, Tim is challenged to become aware of and articulate what God is doing in his life. He needs to discover and discern the call of God in the midst of his apparent pigpen, the loss of interest in spiritual things. In a nutshell, the burden of spiritual direction is on Tim as he struggles to answer the question "What is God up to in my life?" That question, as mysterious as an apparently unanswered prayer, as exhilarating as the arrival of a new child or as riveting as one's first love letter, has been the sole topic of spiritual direction down through the centuries.

HONORING GRACE

Grace—what God is up to in our lives—is like that mysterious impulse that gathers geese in a flock to begin heading south for the winter. It is like the air we breathe in and exhale. It is like that magical, unnoticed moment when the periwinkle suddenly blossoms. When we commit to spiritual direction, we are dedicating and devoting ourselves to a process of attention, discovery and articulation. Spiritual direction is another help along the way to growing in awareness and staying on the path that leads us home.

As the directee, Tim is challenged to make the commitment to spend some time every day being present to the divine Presence. He needs to recognize the action of God in daily events as he becomes aware of that mysterious impulse that entices him to act in this or that way. He also has to become aware of the feelings, reactions and desires of his heart and watch them as they wither or blossom. Having discovered just how real and close God's grace and action are in his life—like the air he breathes—Tim names, celebrates and discusses their implications and challenges with his spiritual director.

As his spiritual director, I accompany Tim on his journey, both as a witness and as a sounding board. No wonder some people prefer to refer to spiritual direction as "spiritual companionship."

Margaret initially was discouraged, lacked confidence and felt that she wasn't following her passion. When she first approached me about beginning spiritual direction, she asked, "Isn't it like life coaching but in a spiritual sense?" I had to disagree. Life coaching is precisely that: having a coach to help one negotiate the hurdles of life. In life coaching, a person discovers what motivates him or her. A person learns how to create a life following his or her passion, priorities and talents. It's about gaining self-confidence, becoming efficient and breaking out of self-defeating behavior.

Spiritual direction, on the other hand, is about committing to the attention, discovery and articulation of something deeper: the reality of God's grace in our lives. Indeed, there is nothing to get in the spiritual life; the challenge is to become aware of what we already have.

So many people miss out on a fuller, more exhilarating dimension of life simply because they iPod their way to work, eyes stuck in today's newspaper. They have only a faint sense, if any, of God's grace dancing and dallying before them in the present moment, inviting them into a homecoming party beyond their wildest expectations. Like geese preparing to migrate, they might be caught up in a daily routine or yearly ritual without any awareness of the mysterious impulse to which they are responding.

Having begun spiritual direction about a year ago, Belinda, now a student enrolled in a college program for adult learners, has discovered the spiritual wisdom in the advice she always gave her children before they crossed the street: "Stop, look and listen." She is the first to admit that it is hard work that demands a commitment of time she sometimes struggles to find in her hectic schedule of a day job and night classes. "But it has opened up a whole new world for me," she says, "and sometimes provides the motivation to wake up on a Monday morning for work or to go to class on a Friday evening. I have come to see that both my job and school are part of a larger hope and future that God has had in store for me."

In just about a year, Belinda has discovered and continues to stand in awe at the way the call of God is sometimes intermeshed and intertwined with her deepest hopes and dreams. And that discerned discovery has happened because every day she takes some time out to "stop, look and listen" as she asks herself the age-old question for spiritual direction: "What is God up to in my life?"

Of course, Belinda is not naive. The commitment to spiritual direction is also hard work, because sometimes when she sits down to ask herself that question, she becomes aware of the false self that vies for her attention and seduces her away from the present moment and down dark alleys she has no business visiting. And so, she notes the presence of the false self, tries to discover what's motivating the journey away from home and learns from her experience.

Speaking of the near occasions of grace, as well as the near occasions of sin, is countercultural. In a world that glibly talks about the weather, the quarterback at last night's football game, the sales at the department stores and the traffic on the way to work, spiritual direction truly stands out as a unique and sacred discussion. It revels in the closeness of God's action in life, even as it reveals some of our less-than-laudatory actions and feelings. Awareness of the struggle between the true and false selves helps provide subject matter for spiritual direction.

WHY DO IT?

So why do ordinary people like Carolyn, Bill, Margaret, Tim and Belinda commit to discovering and articulating God's grace in their lives? There are a number of reasons.

WHY COMMIT TO SPIRITUAL DIRECTION?
• To learn how to be attentive to God's grace in one's life
• To deepen awareness of God's grace
• To explore what obstructs one's attention to God's grace
• To name and honor near occasions of grace
• To find the grace offered in loss, grief, anger or fear
• To be conscious of God's grace in a moment of transition
• To make an important decision in light of God's grace

To learn how to be attentive to God's grace in one's life. Found guilty of heresy and sedition, the Greek philosopher Socrates announced to the jury in Athens, "The unexamined life is not worth living." The blunt wisdom of this certainly gives cause to pause—to stop, look and listen.

People like Tim just are not reflective. Others, especially those going through the midlife transition like Belinda, begin to hunger for a deeper experience of faith. And yet they don't know what to do or how to get there. In spiritual direction, the director can offer suggestions, advice and sometimes even share some time-honored techniques that have helped directees become reflective and grow in sensitivity to God's presence.

Over time, as the spiritual director-directee relationship grows and develops a history, the director also becomes the memory and reminder of how God's grace has touched us in the past. That witness can have a healing effect, as it did in Carolyn's case.

Carolyn had been in spiritual direction for a little over six months. During this particular session, she continued her five-year struggle to make sense of her divorce. It was an agonizing session.

Having come to learn how God and she related to one another, I simply reminded her of what she had said during our very first session: "I really believe that God's ways are not my ways, like the Bible says. Some events just don't make sense to me and that's okay. The more I remind myself of that, the more I find myself growing in trust and surrender." Reminding her of her own words on this particular morning was a moment of grace, surrender and freedom for Carolyn. She's never looked back and has never brought the topic up again.

To deepen awareness of God's grace. Some people are naturally reflective or practice a daily examination of consciousness. Spiritual direction is a time for us to discuss how God is acting in our lives. The very act of naming these occasions of grace is a way of growing in deeper awareness and gratitude for them, as it was in Belinda's case. Francis of Assisi called this attitude of awareness the "spirit of prayer and devotion" and urged his friars never to lose it.

To explore what obstructs one's attention to God's grace. Spiritual direction is not only a time to honor the near occasions of grace in our lives, but also a time to confront the near occasions of sin, namely, the attraction to the Empty Ps and the avoidance of pain, blame, criticism, disgrace and loss.

Tim's apparent loss of faith all started when he occasionally slept in on Sunday mornings and stopped making the effort to go to his usual church service. The attraction to the P of pleasure rears its head in many ways. Tim sometimes promised himself that he would make up for it by attending the Wednesday night service.

That promise often went unfulfilled. With no weekly reminder to honor the Lord's Day, Tim quietly lost touch with God. Early on in spiritual direction, he discovered that he was prone to neglect his relationship with God when productivity was kicking up some dust and things were successfully moving along in his life.

Sometimes we develop habits or deliberately make choices that hinder us from being attentive and freely responding to God's grace in the present moment. Consequently, a spiritual direction session might occasionally include troubleshooting and brainstorming ways to reconcile and rebuild broken bonds with God, others or ourselves.

To name and honor near occasions of grace. This is the heart and soul of spiritual direction. We discover the unconditional lavishness of God's love, presence and grace in the very midst of the daily humdrum of life. Grace is everywhere—it's like the air we breathe and the sunshine we enjoy. The act of articulating and speaking about its presence and action in life becomes an act of adoration.

To find the grace offered in loss, grief, anger or fear. The great Jesuit spiritual director of the seventeenth century, Jean Pierre de Caussade, once wrote to a directee, "Every moment we live through is like an ambassador who declares the will of God." While this is an exhilarating discovery in the midst of love relationships and job promotions, it certainly gives reason for reflection in times of painful separation experienced in deaths, hurricanes and broken hearts. In spiritual direction, we learn the saintly art of surrender and trust in the mystery of grace. Such surrendering trust is characteristic of the true self.

To be conscious of God's grace in a moment of transition. All change is stressful. Moving to another city, changing jobs, having surgery or becoming single naturally raises worries and concerns.

What brought Tim to the first spiritual direction session to discuss his lack of faith was, as I learned before the end of the session, a pending biopsy for cancer. One could go through such experiences with the feeling of being abandoned or forgotten by God. Spiritual direction challenges us to be sensitive to God's grace even in the midst of life's changes and adjustments. It helps us discover the hope found in Julian of Norwich's famous statement "All will be well."

To make an important decision in light of God's grace. As we name and honor the near occasions of grace, we become aware that grace comes with the responsibility of a response. This leads to the topic of discernment, the holy task of deciding how to live life as a dream keeper. Such decisions include lifelong commitments such as marriage or religious life, lifestyle changes, justice issues and involvement in some form of ministry, outreach or apostolic activity. With our spiritual director, we discern and decide how best to respond to God's grace.

Bill had been a successful lawyer for many years. He initially described his personality as "manipulative and ruthless," and added, "I charge for every *second* of my time." That lifestyle returned to him the appearance of the American Dream come true: a large two-story home in the suburbs with a Lexus and SUV parked in the garage. It wasn't rocket science to count the Ps to which he was enslaved.

Once he began developing a reflective lifestyle and talking during spiritual direction about the reality of God's grace in his life, Bill felt the inherent selfishness his lifestyle represented. He needed to do something for others. We discussed a myriad of possibilities. Admitting that he didn't see himself working at a soup kitchen or a homeless shelter, he realized that he could, in his words, "redeem my lifestyle by accepting pro bono cases on behalf of people who could never afford me." And that's exactly how he brings self-emptying love to the profession of law today.

Spiritual direction is a process, and as such, occurs on an ongoing, regular basis. It is not simply a one-time-only discussion. We build a history with our director and in so doing also build up a history of awareness and consciousness to the near occasions of grace offered by God.

WHAT DO WE "DO" IN SPIRITUAL DIRECTION?

We typically meet on a monthly basis with the spiritual director for about one hour. Having prayerfully prepared, we bring to the session thoughts, reactions and issues that have arisen as a result of pondering the daily question "What is God up to in my life?" This could include topics such as prayer, an experience we had during a worship service or liturgy, emerging feelings, an insight we discovered while prayerfully reading Scripture, an experience in our significant relationships, an important decision that needs to be made or challenges in the workplace.

Spiritual direction requires utmost trust. This is essential. An atmosphere of unbridled trust provides the acoustics of freedom and transparency to talk openly and honestly about the near occasions of grace and the near occasions of sin. Spontaneous revelation is an act of reveling and adoration; it can also be an announcement of repentance and the decision to come home.

When Bill first started spiritual direction, with its invitation to a daily examination of consciousness, he was like a kid in a candy store. As his director, I felt privileged to watch this "manipulative and ruthless" man be transformed into a model of generosity and charity in the marketplace. I remember vividly the day he confronted his selfishness and began the discernment process that has

led him to accepting a large number of pro bono law cases. However, more humbling for me was when this man, happily married
for twenty-two years, looked me straight in the eye and said, "I
have never told this to anyone before. But it's time for me to start
addressing my obsession with Internet pornography." I witnessed
a near occasion of grace in that very admission. That single act of
revelation spoke volumes about Bill's trust and openness with me.

Of course, such trust does not happen overnight and is not just
given to any stranger or bystander. It comes slowly, is earned and
is a gift. And if given, the spiritual director considers it a sacred
privilege that can never be justifiably violated, compromised or
taken for granted.

However, paradoxical as it sounds, if that trust never develops,
something is amiss. Holding back thoughts, feelings or issues because of feelings of distrust or fear of condemnation are signs that
we might be ill matched for this particular spiritual director. In
that case, we need to politely end the relationship and go in search
of another spiritual director with whom we can be open and honest. The commitment to becoming aware and articulating God's
grace in our lives is so essential that it overrides any concern about
hurting the director's feelings.

Periodically, perhaps every six months or so, we review the relationship with our spiritual director. We outgrow a spiritual director like we outgrow clothes. Or perhaps the spiritual director, for
whatever reason, feels he or she can no longer be a witness and
companion on our journey home. In either case, the commitment
to spiritual direction can continue with another director.

Having said that, however, changing spiritual directors on a regular basis is also an indication that something is amiss. A level of
sacred intimacy develops over time with the spiritual director that

is truly unique and analogous to no other relationship. Some of us might fear the intensity of such intimacy.

Some of us might fear the recurring exposure of our sinfulness. Most of us have three or four temptations that we often or even consistently give in to. It is humbling to return time and time again to the same near occasions of sin. We might mistakenly think that the spiritual director believes we have no willpower or real interest in repentance. And so, because of the P of pride, we find it easier to start the spiritual direction relationship all over again with a new director.

Like many Christians, Tim thought that spiritual direction was similar to short-term counseling. He was looking for the "trap door into the Promised Land," as he called it, that would open up for him after a few sessions. I had to tell him that he was mistaken; there was no secret passageway home that would instantly transform him into a saint and a churchgoing Christian again. Much to my surprise, Tim decided to continue the commitment to the process of attention, discovery and articulation that would be lifelong. Some people don't.

We can begin spiritual direction at almost any age. Some college students, as they begin taking responsibility for their adult spiritual formation, find the accountability to a spiritual director helpful and challenging. Some people seek out spiritual direction as they begin discerning the future direction of their lives in marriage, in ministry or in the marketplace. Finally, a large group of people, finding themselves in the throes of the midlife transition and realizing the lie and illusion of the false self's agenda, seek out a spiritual director to help find meaning and encouragement in this important and graced stage of life.

Some people, as part of their spiritual formation, design a Rule of Life for themselves. Such a Rule of Life is a commitment and calls for periodic review and accountability. Though we do not necessarily have to be in a spiritual direction relationship to design one, it certainly provides attitudes and actions lending themselves for discussion and reflection during spiritual direction. Ideas for creating a Rule of Life are found in appendix A.

WHO SHOULD NOT COMMIT TO SPIRITUAL DIRECTION

Spiritual direction is not short-term counseling or cheap psychotherapy. And so, people in the throes of any kind of addiction—be it chemical dependency, food, sex, gambling—need to address their addiction first. With Bill's revelation, I encouraged him to find a support group for sex addicts, which he did. Often, once the addiction has been admitted and addressed on an ongoing basis, spiritual direction provides a marvelous complement to any addiction therapy or twelve-step program.

Furthermore, people in need of psychological counseling because of some emotional pain or trauma are not advised to initially seek out spiritual direction. For example, when Jane heard about spiritual direction from a friend, she called and made an appointment with me. After arriving and the customary small talk, she began to pour out her soul to me. She had lost her father, her husband and her job all in the matter of four months. She spent the vast majority of our first time together crying and repeating over and over, "I just don't know what I'm going to do."

My response was as painful for her to hear as it was for me to say. I had to tell her that she was ill suited right then for spiritual direction. I encouraged her to go for counseling instead. Counseling deals with coping mechanisms and making the necessary changes in life, so that the client can function on a daily basis. It is only then that the person has the self-possession to confront the agenda of the false self and the stillness to be present to the divine Presence. Self-possession and stillness are essential qualities for finding one's way home.

CHARACTERISTICS OF A GOOD SPIRITUAL DIRECTOR

One does not choose to become a spiritual director in the same way one chooses a career as a nurse or an architect. It is not a question of reading a few books, maybe even getting some training and then hanging out a shingle that announces "Spiritual Adviser." Rather, it is a calling, a charism, a vocation. It is called forth and validated by others who intuit in this particular person a presence, judgment and heart that knows something of the divine Presence. Throughout the history of Christian spirituality, the one consistent "qualification" as a spiritual director has been the call from others and the trust they hand over.

How do we know if a person is worthy of that trust to become our spiritual director? Four characteristics come immediately to mind.

CHARACTERISTICS OF A SPIRITUAL DIRECTOR
• Ability to listen
• Nonjudgmental
• No anger
• Experience of the midlife transition

First, a spiritual director will have the ability and the passion to be a good, wise listener. We could describe the role of the spiritual director as that of a sacred listener who has box seats for the unfolding symphony of our lives. The director listens with reverence and awe as we highlight and discuss the presence and action of God in our lives. As the director listens, sometimes a probing question will arise to help us fully appreciate the mystery of grace.

A second quality of a good spiritual director is the ability to listen without being judgmental. God acts with each of us in a personalized, individualized way, and the director should have the humility and openness to allow God to be God. In his *Introduction to the Devout Life,* the sixteenth-century spiritual director Francis de Sales makes it eminently clear that the spiritual director must never impede the work of the Holy Spirit or be an obstacle to the directee's freedom. Since each of us walks a different spiritual path, the director is called to affirm—and sometimes confirm or even challenge—our unique journey back home and to highlight potential obstacles and potholes along the way. That can sometimes be easier said than done.

Experience teaches a good director when to speak out and when to respect the unique relationship God has forged with the particular directee. It's not a question of a judgment call. It's all about a call to judgment—knowing when to speak the truth with love and when to maintain reverential silence.

From the fourth-century desert where spiritual direction first began taking shape, we learn that the director should not have an angry personality. Anger distorts openness to our revelation and reveling in near occasions of grace. Angry directors struggle to be objective and humble during the time of sacred listening. Though they might be able to hear what we are saying, they are incapable of wise listening.

I distinctly remember having a spiritual director many years ago who would shift bodily positions and suddenly change the topic as soon as I mentioned the suicide of my father. At first, I found this odd, and I would soon discover this topic was off limits. The upshot was that this director was struggling with anger over the same issue: the premature, sudden and tragic loss of a parent.

And finally, a reputable spiritual director will have experienced the midlife transition. Young spiritual directors might have the training and book knowledge needed to listen to God's grace in our lives. Some, like the great Carmelite spiritual director, John of the Cross, might even have an uncanny wisdom beyond their age. However, such directors are the very rare exception. It's primarily after midlife that book knowledge is augmented with life experience. A spiritual director with the insight and experience of the midlife transition under the belt is a trusted companion.

Ministerial ordination is not a guarantee that one has been given the charism as a spiritual director. Some ordained ministers and priests are so overburdened with the demands of church ministry that they do not have the time to offer themselves as spiritual directors. Furthermore, the history of spirituality attests that many laypeople and women religious have been graced with this gift. Nowadays, some have even gone through one-year and two-year training programs to learn the skills that complement the charism of spiritual direction. We make a mistake to limit the possibilities for spiritual direction simply to ordained clergy. For more ideas about where to find a spiritual director see appendix B.

Spiritual direction has had a long and esteemed history within Christianity. In the twenty-first century, it continues to attract students, medical doctors, postal workers and people from almost every other walk of life. Despite its name, it is not one person directing another. Rather, it is entering into a prayerful conversation to discover, articulate and honor the near occasions of grace that get us out of the pigpen and on the path leading home. In doing that on a regular basis, we grow more attentive to the Holy Spirit who, according to John of the Cross, is the one and only spiritual director.

REFLECTION QUESTIONS

1. Who would make a great spiritual director for me?

2. What reasons for committing to spiritual direction resonate with me?

3. Would it be worthwhile and helpful for me to design a Rule of Life (as outlined in appendix A) for my own spiritual formation? What elements should be included in it?

4. Have I had experiences when people have called forth the ministry of spiritual direction from me? If so, when? How do I feel about responding to that call and ministry?

9

CONTINUING HOME

The Ongoing Work of the Spirit

The process of spiritual growth and maturity—"coming home"—is unlike any other process we experience. In the process of our physical and emotional maturity, we move from infancy to childhood through adolescence to adulthood. Each stage is a step away from total dependence on our parents. The process usually culminates in our moving out of the house and sometimes even far away from home.

In spiritual growth and maturity, however, the journey is just the opposite. Our challenge as adults is to become like children and rediscover our interdependence. We are called to return to the very place we left—the sacrament of the present moment that is the home where our Father waits for us.

Furthermore, spiritual growth is not linear like physical growth. Physical maturity is a process of outgrowing the toys of our childhood and the clothes of our adolescence. We recognize that it's impossible to revert to the past.

In spiritual maturity, however, it's the opposite again. We might commit to a life of daily prayer and gradually find ourselves becoming more prayerful and attentive to God's presence in the here and now. But no sooner do we think we're making real progress in the spiritual life, when suddenly we find ourselves back at square one as we wander off in search of one of the Empty *Ps*. Before long, we're right back in a pigpen. The process of spiritual formation does not guarantee we outgrow our past.

I remember a very committed, sincere spiritual directee speaking of her frustration with coming home to her true self. She said to me, "You know, I've committed so much time and energy to God with apparently little to show for it. I'm beginning to think God is not keeping the other end of the bargain."

"And what's the bargain?" I asked.

"That things go the way they're supposed to go. They don't always seem to.

"That everything in my life as a Christian gets easier. But I feel like they're getting harder.

"That I feel God's presence and love more and more. And often I don't.

"So, don't be offended, but I'm tempted to blame God. I am doing what I think I'm supposed to do, but I'm not sure if God is responding to me. I think God should undergo a quarterly performance review like I get at work."

I easily resonated with her dissatisfaction and disappointment. I remembered how Teresa of Avila, after a bump in the road tossed her from her carriage into a mud puddle, exclaimed, "God, if this is how you treat your friends, no wonder they are so few!"

Who's to blame? Are we or God at fault?

BASIC PRINCIPLES OF SPIRITUAL GROWTH

Like many of us, that spiritual directee of mine seemed to think that living the spiritual life with intentionality would provide immediate results. She believed she could manipulate God's response to her spiritual practices and maybe even buy God's grace. She thought that spiritual growth was a step-by-step, progressive trudge from unsavory sinfulness to stunning sanctity. And that meant there was no going back.

Though the spiritual journey, especially as it was articulated in the sixteenth century by Teresa of Avila and her spiritual director, John of the Cross, has a definite sense of moving forward from darkness into light and from slavery into freedom, its stages are not always experienced as clearly and distinctly as they have been delineated. However, traditionally the terrain of the journey has been mapped into four stages: awakening, purgation, illumination and union. Before explaining the stages, it's best to highlight seven timeless, enduring and unchanging principles of spiritual growth that influence the entire terrain. These principles serve as correctives to the four stages and keep each one of our homecoming parties unique and individual.

SEVEN ENDURING PRINCIPLES OF SPIRITUAL GROWTH

1 Each person's spiritual journey is unrepeatable and unique.

2 God chooses to bow in submission to human free will.

3 God is not bound by or restricted to any "approved" map.

4 The place of divine encounter is right here and right now.

5 The spiritual journey gets more difficult the further along a person travels.

6 The traditional four stages of awakening, purification, illumination and union are more like ongoing, cyclic processes than linear stages.

7 The final destination of the spiritual journey is nowhere but the sacrament of the present moment, the here and now.

Each person's spiritual journey is unrepeatable and unique. God is the initiator of the spiritual journey: "We love because [God] first loved us" (1 John 4:19). The expression and experience of God's love—what God is up to in my life—is called grace. And grace will touch each one of us in a certain way and at a different time. Furthermore, each one of us will respond to grace in our own singular way.

Consequently, God's offer of grace and our response give birth to as many different forms of holiness as there are people in the world: from the political resistance of a Dietrich Bonhoeffer to the selfless acts of charity of a Mother Teresa of Calcutta; from the call to national conversion by a Martin Luther King to the writing of novels by a Flannery O'Connor. One by prayer and contemplation in a monastery; another by heroic witness to a virtue; and still a third by fidelity to marriage vows. Each saint's relationship with God is thoroughly individual and unique; yet, at the same time, together the saints form a real communion. And what unites them is the grace of God that challenges them and lifts each one of them from the pigpen.

God chooses to bow in submission to human free will. God will never violate the gift of free will. God entices. God coaxes. God allures, attracts and invites. But God never forces or coerces.

Over a period of years, some of us gradually develop an interest in the spiritual journey and start to intentionally make our way home. We might make a point of practicing being present to the divine Presence on a daily basis. We might see ourselves making progress and moving forward. We experience the reality of grace at every turn as we live in the present moment. We might commit to some self-emptying act of penance to strengthen our bonds with God, others and self. And then suddenly, by our own deliberate decision, we revert back to our old behavior and become caught up in the false self's attractions and aversions. God will never deny us that choice. And so, once again we are forced to remind ourselves that things are not what they seem to be, and we retrace our steps in the direction of being who God calls us to be, little Christs.

Fence-sitters get stuck and become frozen in one place. Some of us feel the tug of grace to change our lives. We know this or that action must stop. We tell ourselves that we should make greater effort in doing something. We have an inkling that we are imprisoned by the Empty Ps and the avoidance agenda of the false self. And yet we have no motivation to change, and so we choose to stay put in the pigpen. We are like "the lazy person [who] buries a hand in the dish, and is too tired to bring it back to the mouth" (Proverbs 26:15). Sadly, some of us choose life on the sidelines as bystanders.

Jesus reminded one potential follower who wanted to first bid farewell to his family, "No one who puts a hand to the plow and looks back is fit for the kingdom of God" (Luke 9:62). Just like that person, some of us respond to grace, make a move out of the pigpen but then momentarily hesitate or even quickly lose interest. We backtrack and return to the obsessions of the false self. A proverb says it in striking terms: "Like a dog that returns to its vomit is a fool who reverts to his folly" (Proverbs 26:11).

Still others have yet to come to the realization that things are not what they seem to be. They are content to wallow with the pigs. They never get started with the journey home.

Wherever we find ourselves in the midst of these people, God patiently waits and eagerly hopes. God entices. God allures. But God never imposes or strong-arms a response to the invitation. God keeps an eye on the path leading home. God's ears listen for the sounds of those familiar footsteps. And God's arms are anxious to embrace and lead us by the hand into the homecoming party and sacrament of the present moment. But it's up to us to place one foot in front of the other.

God is not bound by or restricted to any "approved" map. The spiritual traditions of Christian mysticism and the institutional church offer important landmarks for the journey home: the need for repentance and penance; growth in the virtues, especially love; and openness to the action of the Spirit, to name just a few. However, when all is said and done, God's grace can instantly change any person's spiritual terrain. God can draw up a new map. In a single instant, responding to grace, Mary of Nazareth was transformed from a maiden into a mother, "for nothing will be impossible with God" (Luke 1:37).

By a mystery known only to God, grace has some of us journeying home slowly and deliberately, plodding along inch by inch, step by step. And yet, others seem to leapfrog home with Olympian speed. One thinks of Thérèse of Lisieux who, before her death at age twenty-four, wrote she had found the "elevator" that lifted her up into the arms of Jesus.

God's grace does not always abide by the traffic laws. God is not bound by Global Positioning Systems or the American Automobile Association's road atlases. Witness how the marginalized, charismatic prophet finds a path to challenge and confront the respected, institutional priest. Grace knows short cuts, back alleys and unmarked roads that lead toward home. God, on occasion, designs detours of which we have no clue. We are lost and find ourselves in the middle of nowhere when we think God must follow an approved or published map. But, Jesus said, "The wind blows where it chooses" (John 3:8).

Furthermore, the history of Christian spirituality clearly attests to the fact that on occasion God's grace picks someone to buck the system with an unparalleled interpretation of the Sermon on the Mount. One thinks of the fourth-century desert fathers and mothers, who went out to live amid sand and stone to escape the scandal of the church snuggling up to society. One thinks of Francis of Assisi's novel approach to the evangelical lifestyle and Clare of Assisi's desire for a life of radical poverty. One thinks of the eighteenth-century Quaker John Woolman, whose witness against slavery helped move the Quakers to be the first religious group in America to outlaw slavery among its membership. One thinks of Dorothy Day's spirituality of peace and justice, which made many a middle-class twentieth-century Catholic uncomfortable. One thinks of the cloistered monk Thomas Merton, who disappointed and disquieted many of his readers with his writings against segregation in the South, the Vietnam War and nuclear proliferation. One thinks of Desmond Tutu, the South African Anglican archbishop and opponent of apartheid. One thinks of the controversial theologians of South America who have brought the gospel of liberation to thousands of Christians in "base communities." When it comes to the spiritual life, God remains as radically free as we are.

The place of divine encounter is right here and right now. This principle makes clear that we do not have to get to a certain stage before we can experience the presence and grace of God. Grace is never achieved or earned. It is given freely and lavishly, right here, right now. Every single moment is a sacrament.

Scripture applies the metaphor of a race to the journey of faith (see 1 Corinthians 9:24; 2 Timothy 4:7; Hebrews 12:1). However, this image could be easily misunderstood. The spiritual journey is not like training for a marathon, where the participants have daily and varied running assignments that physically prepare them for the upcoming twenty-six-mile race. We do not have to build stamina and endurance before starting home. The spiritual journey begins the very instant the hardness of the human heart gives way to God's invitation.

Grace is like the air we breathe. It is within us. It surrounds us. And at any moment, in any situation whatsoever, be it sinful or sanctifying, we can make the choice to respond to this generous gift. God is humble enough and eager enough to meet us wherever we are. And with our response, God's dream becomes reality and we come one step closer to the true self.

The spiritual journey gets more difficult the further along a person travels. This principle challenges the misconception that a committed Christian's life is supposed to get easier and easier.

In his book *The Cost of Discipleship,* published in 1937, Dietrich Bonhoeffer made his famous distinction between "cheap grace" and "costly grace." That distinction speaks directly to this principle. Grace without discipline and self-denial is cheap and an aberration. Authentic grace is costly precisely because it demands a death to the ego and the agenda of the false self. Jesus said, "If any want to become my followers, let them deny themselves and take up their cross and follow me" (Matthew 16:24).

This grace-filled death to self, this self-emptying, is not a one-time affair. It is a continual process that occurs day in and day out. There is no rest area on the journey home. We never get a vacation or sabbatical from it. As we respond to grace on more and more different levels, we see how the agenda of the false self has gotten us off track in a variety of different ways: physical, emotional, psychological and spiritual. And so we are constantly coming back to ourselves at various levels as we realize the depths of the false self's rationalizations and defense mechanisms. Just when we think we are almost home, we realize how far we still have to go.

The traditional four stages of awakening, purification, illumina-
tion and union are more like ongoing, cyclic processes than linear
stages. There is a common misconception that the spiritual journey is a ladder on which we climb higher and higher as we step
from rung to rung. This misconception suggests that each stage of
the spiritual journey has its specific homework and once completed, we graduate to the next level. And with graduation, there
is no backtracking.

Nothing could be further from the truth. The spiritual journey
is more like walking through an intricate, winding labyrinth in
which we sometimes have to return in the direction from where we
just came or even retrace our steps, in order to go forward. Paradoxical as it seems, this actually gets us closer to the labyrinth's
center. Consequently, the four stages are more cyclic than linear.
We could be in a combination of stages, and even all the stages to
some extent, at the same time. Hence, it comes as no surprise that
we might find ourselves back at square one, struggling with the attraction to the Empty Ps. We might be well aware that such entice-
ments cannot give us what we really want. The decision to respond
again to God's grace of conversion is typical of the initial stages of
awakening and purification, which get us out of the pigpen.

And yet, at the very same time, we might be growing in the realization that there really isn't anything more that we need in the
spiritual life since we already have it. This realization, which encourages us to get back on the road leading home, is characteristic
of the stage of illumination. We begin to see how grace is everywhere and every moment is pregnant with the divine Presence.

Even while we are responding to the graces of awakening, purgation and illumination, we might occasionally experience the

presence of God that surrounds us and dwells within. The experience of the immediacy and immanence of the divine Presence is a sign of the unitive stage. We experience more and more the sacrament of the present moment as we get closer and closer to being the person God calls us to be.

The final destination of the spiritual journey is nowhere but the sacrament of the present moment, the here and now. The spiritual journey is a love story of God's hope and dream that we come home. It is recognizing the sacred luminosity of the present moment. Like God, we too dally and dance in the present moment, because there is nothing else to get and there is nowhere else to be. God is here. Grace is here. And when we are here, we are home. "Quickly, bring out a robe—the best one—and put it on him; put a ring on his finger and sandals on his feet. And get the fatted calf and kill it, and let us eat and celebrate; for this son of mine was dead and is alive again; he was lost and is found" (Luke 15:22-24).

How does the journey from the humiliation of a pigpen to the homecoming party where we are given robe and ring unfold in our lives? Mindful of the seven principles of spiritual growth just mentioned, there are, nevertheless, some common landmarks we find along the way home to the true self. Let's take a more in-depth look at the four stages and their landmarks. You will find these in a summary format in appendix C.

THE AWAKENING

Before the journey home begins, we waste time on a wild-goose chase and are filled with anxiety. This one worries about the bank account. Another is overly concerned about image, reputation and popularity. A husband is obsessed with climbing the ladder of success while his wife hungers for affection and attention. A person is out of touch with his or her deepest hopes and dreams while trying to live up to the expectations and demands of others. Life becomes a pressure cooker in which some pleasurable fix is needed to relieve and release nervousness and tension. Control issues abound. All of these are experiences of the false self. Though we might have glimmers that this is a problem, we are certainly not consciously doing anything about it.

And then something happens. God initiates an awakening. This awakening is triggered by an event. It can happen anywhere and at any time. It might be consoling, such as a retreat experience or a moment of reconciliation with God or a family member. It might come under the guise of a threatening experience: a diagnosis of a terminal disease, loss of a job, bankruptcy. It might even occur during an important moment in our lives: graduation, marriage, the birth of a child or the midlife transition, to name a few.

This awakening, in whatever unique form God chooses to use, is characterized by a loss of control. We also begin to realize that life is not simply about "me." It must also include God and others. This realization causes the false self to fidget and squirm.

The emotional pain, caused by this graced moment of losing control and recognizing the need for relationships based on love and not simply use, can provide the needed nudge or push to make us come back to ourselves. We wake up and realize we are in a pigpen. We are not at home and have been trapped in the false self's trappings of success. We begin to question why we wasted so much time avoiding pain, blame, criticism, disgrace and loss.

For a very few people, the awakening is a "road to Damascus" experience. They walk away from it changed forever. It marks a definitive turning point in their lives. However, for the vast majority of us, the awakening is slow and gradual, similar to a morning sunrise. Like the healing of the blind man at Bethsaida, one's vision and focus are only gradually corrected (see Mark 8:22-26).

Some may choose not to respond to the grace of awakening. And so it may have to recur on a number of occasions before God's invitation is accepted. In each and every case, the journey begins the minute these words are spoken: "I will get up and go to my father" (Luke 15:18).

PURGATION

As we accept and respond to the grace of God, we are uplifted from the pigpen. In this second stage of the spiritual journey, purgation begins.

In purgation we respond to the call of moral integration. We take a hard and honest look at the sins we nonchalantly commit and justify. We turn our backs on them as we begin to walk in another direction. This is the literal meaning of *metanoia*, "turning around."

We see just how committed we have been to the pursuit of pleasure, praise, power, prestige, position, popularity, people, productivity, possessions and perfection. We begin to remind ourselves that these Empty Ps are not what they seem to be. They are incapable of filling the hole in the heart. They are lies and illusions.

Moral integration continues as we also look at how much time and energy we've wasted trying to avoid pain, blame, criticism, disgrace and loss. These crosses are meant to be embraced, not rejected. We recognize that surrendering to them shapes us more and more into little Christs. They are the sculptor's chisel calling forth the masterpiece from stone.

The Sermon on the Mount becomes our passport as we leave the foreign land in which we find ourselves and return home. That sermon speaks of God's dream and our roles in it. It calls us to restore broken relationships and strengthen them through prayer, fasting and almsgiving. It challenges us to live in the present and not worry or obsess about tomorrow. Praying over these words of Jesus shows us where and how to reform our behavior and become our true selves.

In the purgative stage our next task is to move beyond child-hood religiosity and adolescent religiosity. In many ways, both of them are expressions of a faith rooted in the agenda of the false self. With the former, we attempt to control God with good deeds: "If I do such-and-such good deed, God will love me and answer all my prayers." With the latter, we decide what God can and must do: "How can God possibly allow all the suffering in the world?" It's the question of the teenager.

In this second stage of the journey, both forms of religiosity must yield to mature faith. Such faith is characterized by trust in God and God's ways. Trust is really where the rubber meets the road. We overcome fears and truly live our faith. Without trust, faith is reduced to an intellectual exercise; with it, faith leaves be-hind the footprints of a prodigal pilgrim on the way home.

The final task is the commitment to daily prayer. Daily prayer is our gift to God. It is also God's gift to us. We meet Jesus in prayer. He becomes our friend, companion and lover. He opens our eyes. He also opens our hearts. And suddenly, we begin to see how our prayer spills over into self-emptying acts of charity and compas-sion. We begin living our prayers.

The prayer of the beginner is often chatty, filled with intellectual words and images. We might have long monologues with God. We might "chew" on a Scripture passage, mining its depths and chal-lenges. We might have a long list of petitions for which we pray. We might even think over the past twenty-four hours and see how

God sent grace and angels into our lives. These kinds of prayer, in which we do all the work, are traditionally known as discursive meditation.

Teresa of Avila makes clear that if we commit to such prayer on a daily basis, within three months, we will find it hard to maintain. Indeed, it will become more and more dissatisfying. We will experience boredom and dryness. And it is precisely at this time that we will be tempted to abandon the practice.

In moments of dryness, we should not allow our prayer to become another P—and it does the minute we turn it into a production for pleasure that is supposed to satisfy ourselves. Prayer is focused on Thee, not "me."

Furthermore, dryness and boredom in prayer are not signs that we are a failure in praying. Rather, they are clear signs that "something's cooking" inside us. They are cyclic recurrences in which God's grace purifies any enduring, interior semblance of the false self. And so we surrender to them in faith and trust.

Our continual response to any form of dryness, aridity or boredom in prayer is fidelity, fidelity, fidelity. We are challenged to stay faithful to the daily practice. Our fidelity is an expression of our trust. It gets us at the station and on the platform where we wait for God's express train called amazing grace.

The beginner's dryness in prayer is actually God's grace and invitation to simpler prayer. John of the Cross offers some signs that the beginner is called to a simpler form of prayer: discursive meditation becomes hard and wearisome; our interior and exterior images of God no longer inspire devotion; we find pleasure in being alone and feel the attraction to wait with "loving awareness of God," without any particular meditation and in inner peace, rest and quietness.

In light of John of the Cross's signs, we must never become a slave to any prayer technique and allow it to get in the way of our relationship with God. And it does, the minute we canonize it as the only way to pray or doggedly crank it out. When that happens, it ends up promoting the productivity agenda of the false self.

As in any other relationship, as we grow and become more and more comfortable with God, we become more and more comfortable with silence. This silence is not empty or dead in any way whatsoever; it is a silence pregnant with a loving history between lover and beloved. And so we should always follow the silence whenever God's grace offers the invitation.

The practice of being present to the Presence is a good technique to use in response to God's invitation to a simpler form of prayer. The loving attentiveness to the divine Presence, challenging as it is, satisfies on a very deep level. It also reveals the light that God keeps lit for us at home.

ILLUMINATION

Deepening sensitivity to the light of God is a certain sign that the spiritual journey continues into the illuminative stage. This sensitivity gives way to the realization that there isn't anything to get in the spiritual life. We've always had that which we sought outside and which can fill the hole in the heart. At this point, we stop looking for God and begin nurturing the awareness and sensitivity to the presence of God within us and in which we dwell.

As we break free of the shackles of the false self and make our way home, the traditional gifts of the Holy Spirit, given at baptism, are experienced in a very real way. These gifts have their scriptural roots in the prophet Isaiah, who describes the spiritual endowment of the promised messianic king (see 11:2). In the Greek Septuagint and Latin Vulgate translations of the Bible, the last gift was translated by two different terms—fear of the Lord and piety—and thus arose the tradition of the seven gifts of the Holy Spirit. These gifts are now experienced in powerful ways and make us aware that the God of all grace dallies and sometimes dances in the here and now.

Wisdom, considered the greatest and most perfect gift, gives us the ability to experience the extraordinary in the ordinary—to see God in a spouse or child, to experience God's presence in something as ordinary as Canada geese flying overhead. *Understanding* is the gift of insight, providing us the ability to read between the lines and know the motivation behind our actions. With *counsel,* we are given the grace to rightly judge how to respond to a situation as a dream keeper, not simply react to it. *Strength* is the vitamin shot that nudges us out of the shadows of self-doubt and releases us from the grip of the false self's aversion to criticism that often keeps us from standing up, speaking out and doing what we know is right. *Knowledge* reminds us that created things cannot fill the hole in the heart and reveals to us that there's more to life than meets the eye. *Fear of the Lord* is the response of wonder and awe to God's presence, action and grace in our lives. The gift of *piety* ignites the fires of the spiritual life and makes us passionate in our attempts to preserve and deepen our love relationships with God and neighbor.

With these gifts, we undertake responsibilities with new zeal. We search for new and creative ways to proclaim the gospel with the enthusiasm of Pentecost. Acts of charity are no longer seen as obligations but rather are natural, spontaneous responses to the need of the present moment. What we "should do" becomes "who we are." We're returning home to the true self.

As we were actively engaged in purging ourselves from the exterior attraction to the false self's agenda in the purgative stage, now in the illuminative stage, the Spirit begins to purge the interior realm of the heart, mind, memory and imagination. Desires and cravings do not command the attention or interest they once did. We no longer find it interesting or amusing to dwell on outlandish fantasies. While we practice being present to the Presence, painful memories might arise and even try to scare us away from the present. But again, our natural, spontaneous response is one of fidelity, fidelity, fidelity.

Furthermore, the guilt we felt about our past sin, characteristic of the beginner, is now transformed into sorrow. As fear of God initially gave rise to guilt, now deepening love gives rise to sorrow. God is forging a deeper relationship in spite of our infidelities.

The Dark Night

At some point, we are called to accompany Jesus on the road to Calvary. He asks, "Are you able to drink the cup that I drink, or be baptized with the baptism that I am baptized with?" (Mark 10:38). Analogous to the cyclic recurrence of dryness and aridity that purifies our prayer in the purgative stage, this experience is radically different and much more intense. It is the great divide. John of the Cross calls it the "dark night."

The dark night is the interior dismantling of all that we hold near and dear. It can be precipitated and experienced in the death of a beloved, a hurricane's destruction of a lifetime of possessions and memories or the humiliating, public exposure of a sin we committed in the past. It can come in the opposition and hatred of others, watching a loved one slowly drift away with Alzheimer's disease or the blatant infidelity of a spouse. Some of us experience it just once in life while others have multiple experiences of it. No

matter the manner or how often this cup of suffering is offered—
it is always "custom-fitted," as my spiritual director is prone to
say—life as we have known it comes to an end.

Pious, upright and wealthy Job is the scriptural figure par excel-
lence of the devastation and deep interior confusion wrought by an
experience of the dark night. He is stricken on four fronts as he
loses his property, his children, his health and his peace of mind.
Unable to make sense of why he is thrust into the darkness of this
midnight, he curses the day of his birth and longs for death to end
his affliction. Maintaining his innocence before his friends, who
insist that this experience is a punishment for his personal wrong-
doing and who call him to repent, Job is simply challenged to accept and surrender to the omniscience and almighty power of God.
His dark night is an interior purging of any and all deep-seated
self-reliance, pride or claims of being a self-made success—in effect, a final purging of "me."

John of the Cross writes that it makes no difference whether a
bird is tied down by a rope or a single piece of thread. In either
case, it is unable to fly away. A dark night cuts any remaining
threads of attachment and avoidance that the false self still uses to
enslave us. Paradoxically, under the guise of a disaster, it is a grace
in disguise. Though we experience the dark night as destroying
"me," in point of fact, it is the transformative grace of Thee. It frees
us for the homecoming party.

In the tenth chapter of book two of his commentary on *The
Dark Night*, John of the Cross uses a masterful analogy to highlight
how an experience of the dark night is truly a grace in disguise. He
notes that a dark night prepares us for union with the divine light,
just as fire prepares wood for transformation.

He notes that fire affects a log in a number of ways. First, the fire dehumidifies the wood, dispelling all its interior moisture that would hinder it from catching fire. Second, the fire turns the log black, making it dark and ugly, and even causes it to emit a bad odor. By completely drying out the wood and charring it, the fire highlights and expels all those qualities of the log that hinder its action. Finally, by heating and enkindling it from without, the fire transforms the wood into itself and makes it as beautiful as itself.

The dark night has a similar effect on us. It purges us from the false self and all that would hinder us from fully experiencing the embrace of the God who comes to meet us right where we are. It not only prepares us for the final transformation but also is itself the very instrument of that transformation. John of the Cross notes that, in the end, the wood is like the fire: it is dry and it dries; it is hot and it gives off heat; it is brilliant and it illumines. In the same way, as a result of a dark night of Calvary, we are transformed into who we are called to be, little Christs, children of God.

Our images of God as loving and compassionate are stripped away during this experience. Deep darkness, confusion and doubt descend on us as they did on Job, and we find no God to whom we can pray. We feel pushed aside and abandoned. We lie in a ditch, half-dead. As little Christs on the cross, we cry out, "My God, my God, why have you forsaken me?" (Mark 15:34).

Of course, God has not abandoned us. The last vestiges of the false God we have constructed during our lives are being smashed. God is replacing our carved images with more accurate reflections of the divine likeness. The living God of all grace is now staking claim on our lives and running toward us in a way we could never before have imagined or experienced.

The duration of the dark night is another great mystery of God. Thérèse of Lisieux experienced it for eighteen months; Mother

Teresa of Calcutta, according to her spiritual directors, experienced it for fifty-one years. Its length has nothing to do with our history or our past sinfulness. It is simply another signpost in the unique relationship that God is forging with us as individuals.

No matter its length, the dark night requires a heroic act of surrender. Fidelity, fidelity, fidelity. We allow it to consume us as wood is consumed with fire. Like Jesus on the cross, we continue to live the teachings of the Sermon on the Mount, and we forgive any whom we might blame for this incident in life. If we surrender, like Job and Jesus, to this passion and crucifixion with faithful trust, in all humility, God will meet us right where we are.

UNION

In moments that occasionally flash and crackle across our lives like lightning in the sky, we suddenly find ourselves wrapped within the bosom of a loving God. And God, our divine companion, shares that very love and life with us on the fourth and final stage of the spiritual journey. We walk hand in hand.

When grace opens us up to the unitive stage, we find ourselves naturally receptive to the thoughts and attitudes of Christ. We deliberately refuse to run after the Empty Ps; we also refuse to utilize the avoidance techniques of the false self. All threads have been cut and we are free. We have great control over our behavior with little or no effort. Our lives are intentionally and naturally lived according to the Sermon on the Mount. Being dream keepers, our self-understanding and identity are blazing with the awareness of being little Christs. Our desires and wills come more and more into communion with God's. We are home. We are who God intends for us to be. We have returned to the true self.

The unitive stage suggests a deep, continuing transformation by

grace. Like Christ's, our lives are placed irrevocably and unequiv-
ocally at the service of God. At deeper and deeper levels, we readily
accept the reminder that Paul offered the church at Philippi to im-
itate the self-emptying of Christ (see Philippians 2:5-11). That
downward mobility keeps us centered here and rooted in the now.
Indeed, we happily become humble, obedient "slaves," not to win
approval but to celebrate who we were born to be. We know in our
bones that it's all about Thee and thee, not "me."

Trials and sufferings are experienced more and more as part of
being one with Christ in his Paschal Mystery. After all, we are little
Christs. Though language is incapable of a rational explanation,
we have an intuitive understanding of Paul's curious statement "I
am now rejoicing in my sufferings for your sake, and in my flesh I
am completing what is lacking in Christ's afflictions for the sake of
his body, that is, the church" (Colossians 1:24). Our daily prayer
and constant joy are the simple surrender of Christ in Gethsemane
to the sacrament of the present moment—"Not my will but yours
be done" (Luke 22:42). Surprisingly, we walk with open hands and
open hearts. Our lifestyles are summed up, "Anything for you,
Lord. Everything for you." Or to quote Francis of Assisi, "My God
and my all!"

Life grows in luminosity as we experience God's presence at the
strangest of times, in the strangest of places. We feel a deep interior
union on occasion. We are God-bearers. We are blazing furnaces.
This interior union is matched by the felt awareness of grace that
surrounds us like the air we breathe. We live moment by moment
in the embrace of a loving God.

We live with the expectation that the union we experience with
God is just a foretaste of the eternal banquet waiting for us in
heaven. We wait peacefully and with joyful anticipation for that

day when God takes us by the hand and leads us into the eternal homecoming party.

Until then, we continue to move in and out of deepening awakenings, the need for purification and experiences of illumination. We are home with God. We are the people God created us to be. We surrender to and abide in the sacrament of the present moment. And we live with the astounding awareness that the light God kept lit for us was with us all the time—even as we wallowed in the pigpen.

REFLECTION QUESTIONS

1. How do I see myself growing in and experiencing the stages of awakening, purgation, illumination and union?

2. What and when was my initial experience of the awakening?

3. What and when was my most recent experience of an awakening?

4. What actions and attitudes must still be purged from my life?

5. How do I experience the gifts of the Holy Spirit in my life?

6. What and when was my experience of a dark night?

CONCLUSION

It was *déjà vu*. Almost thirty years ago, I stood in the same place, facing the front door. This time, however, I was standing behind Luke and Katie. Aiden and Melissa were coming over with two-month-old Stephanie Marie. Though the proud grandparents had seen her on a number of occasions since her birth, it would be my first time.

I smiled broadly when I saw her. Stephanie's thick, red hair made it perfectly clear that she was related to Aiden.

"Aiden," I said, "the apple certainly didn't fall far from the tree."

"You're right," he replied, laughing, "but there's one big difference."

"What's that?"

"She's right at home wherever she is. I'm there at times . . . but am still getting there at other times."

Aiden's comment betrayed the fact that God's grace had brought him a long way over the years. It reminded me that it's a grace to be home like Stephanie Marie—and, surprisingly, it's also a grace to realize I'm not quite there yet, like Aiden. So much of the spiritual life is simply about awareness.

Awareness is the key that opens up the sacrament of the present moment. Unfortunately, somewhere along the line, we lost that key. As a grace that we respond to later in life, we have to practice it. Awareness makes us realize we have wasted so much time and energy on a wild-goose chase that has led us right smack among the pigs. It enlightens the fact that things are not what they seem to be. And it makes us realize that there really isn't anything else to get in the spiritual life.

When we consciously take this key and turn the lock on the here and now, the present moment opens up into a banquet where the divine Presence surrounds us like the air we breathe. Like Stephanie Marie, we suddenly find ourselves carried into a home-coming party prepared by a father who has run down the road to meet us exactly where we are.

Why would we ever want to walk away?

Appendix A

DESIGNING A RULE OF LIFE

A Rule of Life might include the following:

- A period of daily prayer and reflection, which would include asking ourselves, "What is God up to in my life?" This period of daily prayer will help provide the "content" that we bring to a spiritual direction session.

- A weekly worship or liturgical celebration with a Christian community. This provides a reminder that we are part of a larger community of faith that has been given a responsibility by God.

- Nourishing ourselves with the Word of God and the wisdom of writers. Praying with Scripture and spiritual reading provide images and vocabulary that help us speak about the movement of grace in our lives. We might initially start with reading the four Gospels to mine the gold found in the life and teachings of Jesus. After that, we could continue with the letters of Paul or the book of Proverbs. Furthermore, the history of spirituality offers an amazing buffet of literature: the sayings of the desert fathers and mothers, the *Rule of Saint Benedict,* the lives and writings of Francis and Clare of Assisi, the anonymous *Cloud of Unknowing,* Teresa of Avila's *Interior Castle,* the *Imitation of Christ* attributed to Thomas à Kempis, John Bunyan's *Pilgrim's Progress,* Jean-Pierre de Cassaude's *Abandonment to Divine Providence,* Francis de Sales's *Introduction to the Devout Life,* Edward

Taylor's *Preparatory Meditations,* Jonathan Edwards's *Treatise Concerning Religious Affections,* Thérèse of Lisieux's *Story of a Soul,* Richard Baxter's *The Saints' Rest,* Walter Rauschenbusch's *Prayers for the Social Awakening* and Caryll Houselander's *Reed of God.* Modern writers include Thomas Merton, Henri Nouwen, Ruth Haley Barton, Adele Ahlberg Calhoun, Anthony de Mello, Emilie Griffin, M. Robert Mulholland Jr., Richard Rohr, James M. Houston, Ruth Burrows, Basil Pennington, Mary Margaret Funk, David G. Benner, Joan Chittister, Thomas Keating and Paula Ripple.

- Performing self-emptying acts of charity. Grace requires a response in action. Without a sense of mission, we are stunted Christians.

- Making an annual spiritual retreat of two overnights. Lovers and spouses have their nights out. We take vacation time away from our work to regroup and reenergize. A retreat provides the booster shot for our spiritual life, especially when it begins to lose the attention it deserves. If our schedule and budget do not allow for a weekend away, we can take advantage of our church's "At Home Retreat" or the parish mission offered every year.

- Prayerfully preparing for a spiritual direction session by having a specific topic to consider and discuss. The burden of spiritual direction is with us, not with our spiritual director. And so we need to have a sense of what we want to discuss during any session. This, of course, is not to limit or take control of the discussion. Such an attitude can become the death knell of a spiritual direction session. It sometimes happens, though, that a session takes its own twists and turns, with issues not previously thought about or reflected on emerging for discussion.

Appendix B

FINDING A SPIRITUAL DIRECTOR

A good way to begin looking for a spiritual director is by contacting local retreat houses and spiritual life centers run by the local Catholic diocese, the Jesuits or the Cenacle Sisters. Many offer spiritual direction. Convents, friaries, priories and the provincial headquarters of various Roman Catholic and Anglican religious communities can also offer suggestions. Some churches, both Catholic and Protestant, have now even hired trained spiritual directors to be part of their ministerial staff.

The Shalem Institute of Washington, D.C. <www.shalem.org>, the Institute for Spiritual Leadership of Chicago <www.spiritleader.org>, the North Park Theological Seminary of Chicago <www.northpark.edu/sem/>, the Christos Center for Spiritual Formation of St. Paul, Minnesota <www.christoscenter.org> and the Weston Jesuit School of Theology of Boston <www.wjst.edu/academics/ma/index.cfm> have fine reputations for the training of spiritual directors. Each can be helpful in finding a local spiritual director.

Finally, it's worthwhile to pay a visit to the website of Spiritual Directors International <www.sdiworld.org>. It offers an extensive, worldwide listing of registered spiritual directors from different Christian denominations. It also offers some practical advice, including questions to ask any spiritual director we may be considering.

Appendix C

CHARTS AND LISTS

THE GREAT INSIGHT

There is nothing to "get" in the spiritual life because I already have it. I simply need to become aware of what I already have.

CHARACTERISTICS OF THE TRUE SELF

- Relational
- Self-giving
- Unflappable and unthreatened
- Focused on the here and now
- Contemplative approach to life
- Wonder and awe
- Trustful surrender
- Compassionate
- Awareness of being a spoke in the larger wheel of creation
- Passion for peace and justice

THE EMPTY Ps OF THE FALSE SELF

- Pleasure
- Praise
- Power
- Prestige
- Position
- Popularity
- People

- Productivity
- Possessions
- Perfection

AVOIDANCE AGENDA OF THE FALSE SELF

- Pain
- Blame
- Criticism
- Disgrace
- Loss

THE LIBERATING INSIGHT

Things are not what they seem to be.

THE SEVEN DEADLY SINS

- Pride
- Envy
- Anger
- Greed
- Lust
- Gluttony
- Sloth

DISTRACTIONS WHILE BEING PRESENT TO THE PRESENCE

- Idle daydreaming
- Emotionally charged thoughts
- "Eureka!" breakthroughs
- Self-reflection
- Interior purification

Components of Discernment

- A person's past history
- A person's potential
- A person's present identity
- A person's hopes, dreams and desires
- A person's baptismal commitment

Why Commit to Spiritual Direction?

- To learn how to be attentive to God's grace in one's life
- To deepen awareness of God's grace
- To explore what obstructs one's attention to God's grace
- To name and honor near occasions of grace
- To find the grace offered in loss, grief, anger or fear
- To be conscious of God's grace in a moment of transition
- To make an important decision in light of God's grace

Characteristics of a Spiritual Director

- Ability to listen
- Nonjudgmental
- No anger
- Experience of the midlife transition

Seven Enduring Principles of Spiritual Growth

1. Each person's spiritual journey is unrepeatable and unique.

2. God chooses to bow in submission to human free will.

3. God is not bound by or restricted to any "approved" map.

4. The place of divine encounter is right here and right now.

5. The spiritual journey gets more difficult the further along a person travels.

6. The traditional four stages of awakening, purification, illumination and union are more like ongoing, cyclic processes than linear stages.

7. The final destination of the spiritual journey is nowhere but the sacrament of the present moment, the here and now.

THE SPIRITUAL JOURNEY

Awakening
- Triggered by an event characterized by loss of control
- Realization that one is in a pigpen

Purgation
- Moral integration
- Mature faith
- Daily prayer

Illumination
- Deepening sensitivity to God's presence in the present moment
- Experience of the seven gifts of the Holy Spirit
- Undertake responsibilities with the zeal of Pentecost
- Holy Spirit cleanses heart, mind, memory and imagination
- Guilt transformed into sorrow

The Dark Night
- Interior dismantling of all that we hold near and dear
- Final purification before the homecoming party
- Images of God are stripped as we feel abandoned

Union
- Naturally receptive to the thoughts and attitudes of Christ
- Freedom from the Empty Ps and false self's avoidance techniques

- Communion with God
- Transformation by grace
- Self-emptying
- Identification with suffering of the Paschal Mystery
- Surrender to the present moment
- Awareness of God's presence like the air we breathe

NOTES

Chapter 1: The True Self

page 21   "For then the soul": Catherine of Siena, *The Dialogue,* trans. Suzanne Noffke, O.P. Classics of Western Spirituality (New York: Paulist Press, 1980), p. 27.

page 25   It's not about me, but about thee and Thee: Albert Haase, O.F.M., *Instruments of Christ: Reflections on the Peace Prayer of Saint Francis of Assisi* (Cincinnati: St. Anthony Messenger Press, 2004).

Chapter 2: The False Self

page 40   In his great work on spiritual growth: John of the Cross, *The Ascent of Mount Carmel,* in *The Collected Words of St. John of the Cross,* trans. Kieran Kavanaugh, O.C.D., and Otilio Rodriguez, O.C.D. (Washington, D.C.: ICS Publications, 1991), pp. 132-33.

Chapter 3: Coming Back Home

page 59   The fourth-century desert tradition: A paraphrase of a story in *The Desert Fathers,* trans. Helen Waddell (New York: Vintage Spiritual Classics, 1998), p. 117.

page 61   A story paraphrased from Portia Nelson's: Original paraphrase found in Noah Levine, *Against the Stream: A Buddhist Manual for Spiritual Revolutionaries* (New York: Harper Collins, 2007), pp. 105-6.

page 68   "Late have I loved you": *Augustine of Hippo: Selected Writings. The Classics of Western Spirituality,* trans. Mary T. Clark (Mahwah, N.J.: Paulist Press, 1984), p. 144.

page 69   "You have made us for Yourself": Augustine *Confessions,* bk. 1, par. 1.

Chapter 8: The Spiritual Director

page 134   "spirit of prayer and devotion": *Francis and Clare: The Complete Works,* trans. Regis J. Armstrong, O.F.M. Cap., and Ignatius C. Brady, O.F.M., Classics of Western Spirituality (New York: Paulist Press, 1982), p. 140.

page 135   "Every moment we live through": Jean-Pierre de Caussade, *Abandonment to Divine Providence,* trans. John Beevers (New York: Image Books, 1975), p. 50.

Chapter 9: Continuing Home

page 158   "loving awareness of God": *The Collected Works of St. John of the Cross,* trans. Kieran Kavanaugh, O.C.D., and Otilio Rodriguez, O.C.D. (Washington, D.C.: ICS Publications, 1991), pp. 189-90.

page 160   The gift of *piety* ignites the fires: Albert Haase, O.F.M., and Bridget Haase, O.S.U., *Enkindled: Holy Spirit, Holy Gifts* (Cincinnati: St. Anthony Messenger Press, 2001), pp. 15-55

page 162   fire affects a log: *Collected Works of St. John of the Cross,* pp. 416-17.

For more information about Albert Haase, O.F.M.,
and his ministry of the Word,
visit his website at <www.AlbertOFM.net>.

formatio
TRADITION. EXPERIENCE.
TRANSFORMATION.

Formatio books from InterVarsity Press follow the rich tradition of the church in the journey of spiritual formation. These books are not merely about being informed, but about being transformed by Christ and conformed to his image. Formatio stands in InterVarsity Press's evangelical publishing tradition by integrating God's Word with spiritual practice and by prompting readers to move from inward change to outward witness. InterVarsity Press uses the chambered nautilus for Formatio, a symbol of spiritual formation because of its continual spiral journey outward as it moves from its center. We believe that each of us is made with a deep desire to be in God's presence. Formatio books help us to fulfill our deepest desires and to become our true selves in light of God's grace.